Neuro-Linguistic Programming in Alcoholism Treatment

ALL HAWORTH BOOKS & JOURNALS
ARE PRINTED ON CERTIFIED
ACID-FREE PAPER

Neuro-Linguistic Programming in Alcoholism Treatment

Edited by
Chelly M. Sterman, MSW, ABECSW, CAC

Routledge
Taylor & Francis Group
LONDON AND NEW YORK

First published 1990 by The Haworth Press, Inc.

2 Park Square, Milton Park, Abingdon, Oxon OX14 4RN
711 Third Avenue, New York, NY 10017, USA

Routledge is an imprint of the Taylor & Francis Group, an informa business

First issued in paperback 2016

ISBN 978-1-56024-002-0 (hbk)
ISBN 978-1-138-97699-3 (pbk)

Library of Congress Cataloging-in-Publication Data

Neuro-linguistic programming in alcoholism treatment / edited by Chelly M. Sterman.
p. cm. – (Haworth series in addictions treatment ; v. 3)
Included bibliographical references.
1. Alcoholism – Treatment. 2. Neurolinguistic programming. I. Sterman, Chelly M. II. Series.
RC565.N36 1990
616.86'106 – dc20 90-34784
CIP

It is my privilege to dedicate this monograph to my mentors, not only for what they taught me, but for what they encouraged me to learn.

With love to Lance, Ilana, and my mother.

ABOUT THE EDITOR

Chelly Sterman, MSW, ACSW, ABECSW, CAC, has worked in the field of alcoholism for 17 years. She is a faculty member of Rutgers School on Alcohol and Drug Studies and of Glassboro College Alcoholism Institute. As a Master Practitioner in Neuro-Linguistic Programming, Ms. Sterman runs a private practice in New Jersey, counseling individuals, couples, and families affected by alcoholism and other addictions. She has developed and presented workshops on rapport skills in addiction treatment, confrontation and conflict resolution, and denial and resistance as strategic treatment tools. She was Chairperson of the New Jersey Alcoholism Counselor Certification Board for two years, conference Co-Chair of the New Jersey NASW Three Day Institute on Alcoholism in 1989, and she presently serves on the Rescue Mission Advisory Board in Trenton, New Jersey. She has also been consultant to the New Jersey Division of Alcoholism, New Jersey Division of Narcotics and Drug Abuse Control, Department of Human Services, Division of Mental Health and Hospitals, Paul Kimball Hospital, IBM Corporation, and Pennsylvania Department of Parole and Probation, as well as various school systems and conferences.

Ms. Sterman received her MSW from University of Kentucky and became a Certified Master Practitioner in Neuro-Linguistic Programming in 1987.

CONTENTS

Contributors

Chelly M. Sterman, MSW, ABECSW, CAC, Master Practitioner in Neuro-Linguistic Programming, has worked in the field of alcoholism for seventeen years. For six years, she was on the New Jersey Alcoholism Counselor Certification Board, two years as its chairwoman and two years as a national board member of the Certification Reciprocity Consortium.

Presently in private practice with two associates near Princeton, New Jersey, Ms. Sterman has worked in a variety of alcoholism and other drug abuse treatment modalities. Ms. Sterman provides individual, couples, and family counseling with a focus on alcoholism and other addictions. She has developed and presented numerous workshops for social service agencies, addiction treatment centers and various states such as New Jersey, New York, Pennsylvania, Iowa and Kentucky for departments such as the Division of Alcoholism and Substance Abuse Control, the Administrative Offices of the Court and Departments of Parole and Probation. These workshops and presentations focus on alcoholism and substance abuse treatment, particularly on clinical issues concerning denial, resistance and confrontation strategies. She is a consultant and supervisor for professionals working in the field of addiction and has been a faculty member of the New Jersey Summer School of Alcohol and Drug Studies for several years as well as the Glassboro College Alcoholism Institute. Ms. Sterman teaches NLP adaptations to addiction treatment at the Eastern NLP Institute.

Eileen Isaacson, MSW, EdD, CAC is a co-founder of the Brunswik Group in New Jersey, providing counseling and consulting services in addiction. She has worked in prevention, clinical treatment and program administration in the areas of addiction and mental health. Her work includes individual, group and family therapy. Dr. Isaacson has developed counselor training programs and supervised professionals working in chemical dependency. She is a faculty member of the University of Rutgers Summer School of Alcohol Studies and the New Jersey Summer School of Alcohol and Drug Studies. Her training includes Neuro-Linguistic Programming (NLP) and hypnosis with Linda Somers, Richard Bandler and Robert Dilts at N.L.P. Eastern Institute, Transactional Analysis with Ed Reese at the N.J. Institute for T.A. and Gestalt and Behavior Modification with the late Frances Cheek, PhD at the NJ Neuropsychiatric Institute.

Donald I. Davis, MD is a Clinical Professor of Psychiatry at the Medical School of George Washington University, and is an Adjunct Professor in the Department of Family and Child Development at the Virginian Polytechnic Institute and State University. Dr. Davis, who is a psychiatrist, is Director of the Family Therapy Institute of Alexandria and is a clinician of the highest caliber in his field. He has published widely about family therapy in the prestigious *Journal of Psychiatry* as well as extensively in book form. In the Washington area, Donald Davis presents as well as sponsors significant conferences which frequently focus on Neuro-Linguistic Programming as a treatment modality for troubled families such as those entrenched in alcoholism.

Jeffrey M. Doorn, MA, CAC is an associate and consultant with the Center for Family Communication, 26 Park Street, Montclair, N.J. He is an adjunct instructor at Jersey City State College and is a co-founder of the Northern New Jersey Study Group on Ericksonian Hypnosis.

James O. Henman, a licensed psychologist, received his PhD in Clinical Psychology from the California School of Professional Psychology at Fresno in 1978. He was the Director of the Family Service Agency of Stanislaus County from 1971 to 1976.

In addition to a full-time practice since 1976, he teaches clinical courses on a part-time basis at California State University, Stanislaus and consults with the Chemical Dependency Unit of Modesto Psychiatric Center.

He developed the therapeutic approach Cognitive-Perceptual Reconstruction as an outgrowth of working extensively with adult children over the past 17 years. He has been actively working on his own recovery as an adult child of dysfunction since 1977.

Sonia M. Henman, a Marriage Family Child Counseling intern,

received her Master's of Science in Counseling Psychology in 1987 at California State University, Stanislaus. She is currently working at the Family Service Agency of Stanislaus County and is in part-time private practice at Psychological Associates in Modesto.

She has also been a licensed registered nurse since 1977. She has worked in hospital settings and as a pediatric nurse.

She teaches on a part-time basis for the Psychology Department at California State University, Stanislaus. She has been an active participant in developing the therapeutic approach of Cognitive-Perceptual Reconstruction.

Matthew Tierney is currently director of the Wayne Institute of New Resources, Wayne, New Jersey. Mr. Tierney completed the Training Program for Alcoholism Counseling, through the West-chester Council on Alcoholism, White Plains, New York in 1981. Since then he has maintained a private practice specializing in alcoholism/substance abuse counseling and counseling adult children of dysfunctional households. He is also a master hypnotherapist and an international trainer of Neuro-Linguistic Programming.

Mr. Tierney has served as a Rehabilitation Consultant to such organizations as Southern Institute of NLP and Eastern Institute of NLP. He has also worked as a traumatic stress consultant to fellow Vietnam War Veterans.

In recent years, Mr. Tierney has lectured to diverse groups on the application of Neuro-Linguistic Programming in the treatment of alcoholism and substance abuse. Included among the lecture groups are the University of Miami, Fordham University, and the 1986 National Conference for Substance Abuse Counselors.

Dr. Ann Gardner is a Developmental Psychologist (PHD, University of North Carolina-Chapel Hill, 1972) with 15 years of experience in the Human Services field. She was Assistant Professor of Psychology (1971-1974) and then a member of the adjunct faculty (1974-1980) at Emory University in Atlanta, Georgia. Since 1974 she has worked primarily as a consultant. She is currently an NLP Trainer and therapist and an independent consultant to corporations and governmental agencies in New York City.

Preface

Gail Gleason Milgram, EdD

Alcoholism is a major societal problem in the USA; health care costs, accidents, and lost productivity have been estimated to be over 100 billion dollars a year. The disease of alcoholism negatively impacts the alcoholic individual, his/her spouse, children, friends, co-workers, the community, and society in general. Alcoholics experience physical, mental, emotional and social problems which create dysfunction in their lives and those of significant others. Countering the devastation of the disease is the hope offered by treatment. Individuals can recover and lead healthy and productive lives; families are able to develop positive and helpful dynamics; and recovering alcoholics do return to work as responsible and dependable employees. Alcoholism treatment is available throughout the United States in a variety of settings (residential treatment facilities, out-patient clinics, hospitals, etc.). These settings are staffed by alcoholism counselors who are trained to help patients during the intervention, treatment program, and the recovery process.

The significance of an "extensive repertoire of treatment skills, strategies, and techniques which match the needs of alcoholic clients and their families" is noted by Chelly Sterman in Chapter 1. Insight is provided on the historical development of Neuro-Linguistic Programming (NLP) and its goal to generate internal choices in the client. NLP enables the therapist to expand his/her existing skills and create additional strategies in order to increase the effectiveness of treatment. Being able to "read" the client is an important dimension of the therapeutic process; it allows the therapist to study the structure of subjective experiences and the limits these impose on the individual. By facilitating the development of internally generated choices, the individual is able to construct alternate methods of dealing with the world.

Eileen Isaacson provides a foundation for NLP in her review of the existing literature in Chapter 2 and describes NLP as a model that elicits information from the subjective representational sensory systems and which directs its strategies to the conscious and unconscious processes of the addicted individual. She emphasizes the interplay between the epistemology of addiction, and the skill base in eliciting information related to the individual's behavior in response to the drug, significant others, and the environment. Using case histories, Dr. Isaacson demonstrates some basic NLP assumptions and a specific NLP technique, the six-step reframe.

In the third chapter, Chelly Sterman elaborates on creating rapport with clients, which is a significant factor of NLP. An understanding of the alcoholic client's model of the world is described by means of eye and speech patterns. The concepts for establishing a therapeutic relationship (e.g., translating, anchoring, and outcome framing) are also discussed.

Donald Davis focuses, in Chapter 4, on NLP and the family in alcoholism treatment, particularly the essential family tasks to be accomplished in successful pre- and post-treatment. Davis clearly demonstrates how NLP offers a variety of methods of assisting in the accomplishment of these tasks and discusses NLP's premise that each family system contains the necessary resources that are required to complete these tasks. Davis further demonstrates how rapid change in alcoholic family systems may be accomplished through the NLP skills and strategies, especially by using swish patterns, phobia frames and changes in limiting beliefs through work with submodalities. This chapter is followed by Jeffrey Doorn's writing on Ericksonian hypnotherapy, which made a major contribution to NLP. Doorn emphasizes the successful integration of the resistant client into the treatment experience, utilizing resistant responses consistently to further the alcoholic client's internal resource building. Doorn describes eliciting cooperation, utilizing resistance, building choices, and assigning tasks via case demonstrations.

Ms. Sterman, Chapter 6, demonstrates the six-step reframe, which is a specific NLP technique; she describes its use as a negotiation model using both conscious and unconscious resources to motivate the alcoholic client's movement toward health. Emphasis is placed on accessing the alcoholic's internal resources and negotiating a compromise with internally conflicting parts, as clarified by several case demonstrations.

Chapter 7 is written by Sonia and James Henman, who term their form of alcoholism treatment "Cognitive-Perceptive Reconstruction." In addition to NLP, they include several approaches to psychotherapy under a spiritual umbrella. Special emphasis is placed on reconnecting the internal child to the adult organism; this is demonstrated through several case examples including descriptions of working with partners of alcoholics, as well as Children of Alcoholics (COAs).

This chapter is followed by Ms. Sterman's "Role of Sorting Mechanisms and Basic Human Programs in the Treatment of Alcoholism." Sorting mechanisms are described as the ways in which alcoholics and alcoholic family systems create order in their model of reality; these are the essential skills in creating individuals' basic human programs such as motivation, decision-making and learning. Each description of a sorting skill and basic human program is accompanied by one or several case demonstrations. Chapter 9, written by Matthew Tierney, addresses itself to the chronic alcoholic and dually addicted individual and offers a positive NLP framework for coping with this specific category of addicts. A great deal of flexibility and emphasis on the need to meet the alcoholic client in his model of the world is noted. The client's ability to learn to take personal responsibility for his/her experience is discussed as essential. Tierney perceives NLP as going beyond symptom removal; it is designed to change the alcoholic's behavior by changing his/her internal perceptual structure.

In the following chapter, Ann Gardner specifically focuses on the contribution NLP is making to the issue of co-dependency. Giving several examples, Gardner describes a variety of characteristics attributed to co-dependent individuals and applies Robert Dilt's template for limiting beliefs to these characteristics in COAs. She discusses the NLP meta programs as a foundation for intervention in co-dependent systems and gives an NLP treatment format for integrating conflicting beliefs; she also describes the reimprinting process. Ms. Gardner further discusses NLP's use of major COA issues such as loss, trust, and intimacy.

This book is a clearly written guide to the use of Neuro-Linguistic Programming in the treatment of alcoholism and other addictions. NLP's focus on the individual and the family increases the effectiveness of counseling by targeting the uniqueness of each individual and his/her family system. Clear, extensive case demonstrations of NLP techniques, skills and strategies are interspersed throughout the text. In the final chapter, Ms. Sterman provides an extensive and up-to-date annotated bibliography of NLP publications.

Alcoholism treatment has benefited from NLP contributions. NLP facilitates effective interventions, helps clients develop internal resources, creates individualized treatment and enhances the recovery process. NLP also helps clinicians feel more confident with their skills. Since NLP's focus is on moving the client toward a state of well-being by means of specific techniques and strategies, the counselor's effectiveness is increased. NLP's principle that a person naturally moves toward well-being supports the need for the counselor and the client to work to generate new choices. NLP is a form of psychotherapy that helps alcoholics create internal coping skills to begin and maintain the process of recovery.

Gail Gleason Milgram, EdD
Professor/Director of
Education & Training
Center of Alcohol Studies
Rutgers University

Introduction

Chelly M. Sterman, MSW, ABECSW, CAC

In the summer of 1987, faculty members at the Rutgers Summer School of Alcohol and Drug Studies were discussing clinical advances in the treatment of alcoholism and substance abuse. Some of the faculty members were aware that I had made a special study of Neuro-Linguistic Programming since 1983 and began addressing the NLP techniques as applicable to the field of addiction treatment. I wistfully stated that at a future time I would like to write about Neuro-Linguistic Programming and its use in the treatment of addictive systems. That was when I met Bruce Carruth, then editor of *Alcoholism Treatment Quarterly*, published by The Haworth Press, who suggested the following writings. Prior obligations prevented the actual project to be started until January of 1988, but all through these months it was exciting to discover colleagues who had begun to experiment and be successful at using some of the skills and strategies described in this book.

My friend Eileen Isaacson focused on eliciting information from the subjective representational sensory systems in alcoholic and otherwise addicted subjects, and connecting this to desired outcomes. I was fortunate to find Dr. Donald Davis willing to contribute a chapter on the use of NLP techniques in alcoholic family systems. Having known Jeffrey Doorn for several years as an accomplished alcoholism counselor, I was pleased to receive his chapter on hypnotherapy in the Milton Erikson tradition, which was the most powerful precursor of Neuro-Linguistic Programming. Reading through *Focus* magazine, I found an article by James Henman which described treatment of Adult Children of Alcoholics (ACOAs) in NLP terminology. After contact was made, it was delightful to work with Dr. Henman and his wife Sonia, and receive their chapter "Cognitive-Perceptual Reconstruction in the Treatment of Alcoholism." I had the good fortune to meet two skillful and knowledgeable therapists in the addiction field during my own NLP training. They each contributed a chapter in the area of their expertise, Matthew Tierney in "Neuro-Linguistics as a Treatment Modality for Alcoholism and Substance Abuse," and Ann Gardner who wrote "An NLP Perspective on Co-Dependency."

Writing the book was a truly valuable experience and collaborating with six authors who each contributed a chapter was a joy as well as a challenge. It was exciting to find so many good counselors and therapists who were involved in the treatment of alcoholism and other addictions experimenting with novel techniques such as NLP.

My life has been enriched through the contact with all those involved in the writing of this book as well as by the discipline involved in formulating, expressing, and evolving my own thoughts regarding NLP and alcoholism and other addiction treatment.

This has been especially significant when training alcohol and other addiction counselors in the skills and strategies of Neuro-Linguistic Programming as well as teaching NLP students about alcoholism and other addictions at the Eastern NLP Institute.

I am indebted to Linda Sommer, my NLP trainer and director of the Eastern NLP Institute.

A special thanks goes to my daughter, Ilana, who did my typing and editing, and took care of my occasional lapses into bad grammar. She was a gracious assistant.

It is truly my hope that the content of this book will create the context for further innovations in the treatment of alcoholism and other addictions.

Chapter 1

Neuro-Linguistic Programming as a Conceptual Base for the Treatment of Alcoholism

Chelly M. Sterman, MSW, ABECSW, CAC

INTRODUCTION

The title of this monograph, *Neuro-Linguistic Programming in Alcoholism Treatment*, indicates that this work has been written with the intent of adding choices to the collection of treatment modalities in the field of alcoholism and other addictions, a field that has undergone such a rapid expansion over the past twenty years.

The purpose of Neuro-Linguistic Programming is to reflect, as an individualized rather than general process, the needs of each client, and to have the capability to respond with treatment that specifically addresses these clients' unique needs. An expression of this concept, "The way you holler up the mountain is the way your echo comes back to you," accurately represents this concept.

As a therapist, having worked in the field of alcoholism for over fifteen years, the significance of an extensive repertoire of treatment skills, strategies, and techniques which matches the needs of alcoholic clients and their families has time and again presented itself. Even though individuals as well as families involved in an alcohol addiction process have many commonalities it is equally true that each individual has his own set of fingerprints, his uniqueness as a human being. Therefore, the more treatment can be directed specifically to a particular alcoholic individual or family, taking both generalities as well as individualizations into consideration, the more effective alcoholism counseling is. If "hollerin' up the mountain" is the therapist's set of treatment interventions, and if "the echo" is the result, the outcome of these interventions for the client, the contribution NLP makes to alcoholism treatment is the creation of a requisite variety of "hollering" adapted most accurately to the desired "echoes."

The purpose of NLP is not to replace any existing knowledge or effective treatment methods of therapists, but to add to the therapists' existing repertoire of treatment modalities in order to create an extensive set of skills and strategies for increasing this effective treatment. NLP has very little content beyond some basic beliefs about human values and complete respect for each client. It primarily has a process orientation, which makes it exquisitely adaptable to the framework within which each individual therapist functions. In the five years that I have applied the NLP skills both to the treatment of alcoholic individuals as well as to the extensive training of alcoholism counselors, I have always found a real match with any concurrent treatment philosophy. In other words, NLP's process orientation allows for a complete integration with preexisting frameworks clients and counselors have used to obtain and maintain sobriety.

HISTORICAL BACKGROUND

According to its founders, Richard Bandler and John Grinder, NLP as a therapeutic process was originally in part based on the psychological, emotional, or behavioral developments of three recent great innovators in the field of psychotherapeutic treatment, and in part on these individuals' personal style and almost magic ability to heal their clients. These people were Virginia Satir with her great innovations in the field of family therapy, Fritz Perls, the father of Gestalt Therapy, and Milton Erickson, who made some of the most significant contributions to hypnotherapy, the exquisite marriage between hypnosis and therapy which allows for full use of all available conscious and unconscious resources of human beings.

In examining the different systems of treatment, Bandler and Grinder found much that explained the healing qualities of these therapies, but did not account entirely for the great success these individuals personally achieved in their own work with clients. The founders of what became NLP examined the styles of these three masters and discovered a number of commonalities which were, until then, largely ascribed to "intuition." All three apparently had exquisite ways of "reading" the client—what NLP later called "calibration"—on a less than conscious level, even before the client was aware of particular "cues" in himself. One of these "discoveries" involved "eye patterns." Some other commonalities involved what NLP calls the meta-model, specific use of rapport skills, and use of language, particularly predicates, and somewhat later on, the use of submodalities. In this chapter, some of these elements will be demonstrated in relation to their use in alcoholism treatment, some will be extensively examined in other chapters and for some a referral will be made to the literature described in this monograph's bibliography.

Steve Andreas, in *Frogs Into Princes*, states:

> In one sense, nothing that NLP can accomplish is new. There have always been "spontaneous remissions, miracle cures and other sudden and puzzling changes in people's behavior and there have always been people who somehow learned to use their abilities in exceptional ways. What is new in NLP is the ability to systematically analyze these miracles and use these strategies to implement them in individuals who for some reason do not have spontaneous access to these resources.[1]

NLP has made substantial inroads in making strategies, skills and techniques available that used to be considered magical or intuitive.

RATIONALE

Neuro-Linguistic Programming (NLP) presents itself as an artful technology for studying the structure of subjective experience and the limitations these subjective experiences impose on each individual. With as much precision and reliability as is available to this young field today, NLP has developed methods, skills, and strategies for increasing and expanding these internal representations of human beings to allow for the construction of an effective repertoire of internally generated choices in people's multitudinous life situations.

As is the case with any major dysfunction or illness, alcoholism, or the process of being an alcoholic, erodes this internal repertoire of choices, until life becomes determined by basically one primary factor: access to alcohol. Stated in a different way, the use of alcohol determines the lifestyle of an alcoholic, imposing severe limitations on the individual's subjective experience. Thus, presently existing treatment modalities such as inpatient treatment day programs, Alcoholics Anonymous (AA), etc., are appropriately geared toward dealing with individuals whose internal choices have been brought to a minimum. Each successful program provides a firm, clear structure with plentiful information on "how to" restart life in the context of nil-choice. Each program not only teaches lifeskills, but also specific values and beliefs and proclaims the absolute necessity for clients to live their lives by these beliefs. One frequently hears when an alcoholic has a slip: "If only he had—gone to a meeting—taken one day at a time—followed: easy does it—listened to his sponsor—turned it over (to God), etc."

All of the above, of course, is true, and the recovering alcoholic knows this as well as anybody else. Why then do some follow paths that lead back to alcohol abuse and to pain, often destruction? NLP believes that the answer lies in internal lack of choices and that the bridges from alcoholic drinking "to getting sober" to "staying sober" is the creation of sufficient internal variety of coping skills. Thus, NLP presents methods for constructing individual's unique, distinctive internal road maps for dealing with the world. The belief of each individual's uniqueness, his set of fingerprints is the basis for NLP's treatment modes. The therapist discovers how his clients receive, filter, and organize sensory information in the cognitive-perceptual patterns that result in emotions and behavior. NLP is in the process of developing "technology" for therapists to deliberately internally "install" various processes, allowing individuals "requisite variety," the choices needed for that person to move toward well being in a consistent way, having the means to internalize all the appropriate information he learns during his ongoing recovery process.

NLPs BASIC CONTRIBUTION

NLP, though presently expanded to an extensive set of contextual beliefs about human beings with an ever-increasing repertoire of specific skills and strategies geared toward moving clients toward their compelling futures, has two basic premises for calibrating information and then using this information in "designer" treatment modes.

The first discovery involves the pattern of eye movements. In *Applications of Neuro-Linguistic Programming*, Robert Dilts states:

> Human beings reflect their internal sensory processes not only by the sensory-based words that they us, but also by certain behavioral cues. Eye movement patterns are one of the most readily detectible behavioral cues. The following eye-movement patterns in most right-handed individuals are indicative of the following internal processing.
>
> Eyes up and to the left . . . remembered imagery(Vr)
> Eyes up and to the right . . . constructed imagery(Vc)
> Eyes defocused . . . unspecified imagery
> Eyes down and to the left . . . internal dialogue(Ad)
> Eyes level to the left . . . remembered dialogue (Ar)
> Eyes level to the right . . . constructed sounds(Ac)
> Eyes down and to the right . . . kinesthetics (feelings, emotions) (K)[2]

A simplified visual representation is shown (see Figure 1).

What is the significance of this discovery for the treatment of alcoholism. To illustrate, a couple of small vignettes are presented here:

1. A counselor asks an alcoholic who has completed three weeks of treatment in an inpatient program, where he will go after his discharge. Before the client answers, the counselor sees rapid eye movement in the visual sphere, from remembered to constructed, back and forth several times, and then the eyes move to down right at which point he dejectedly answers, "I don't

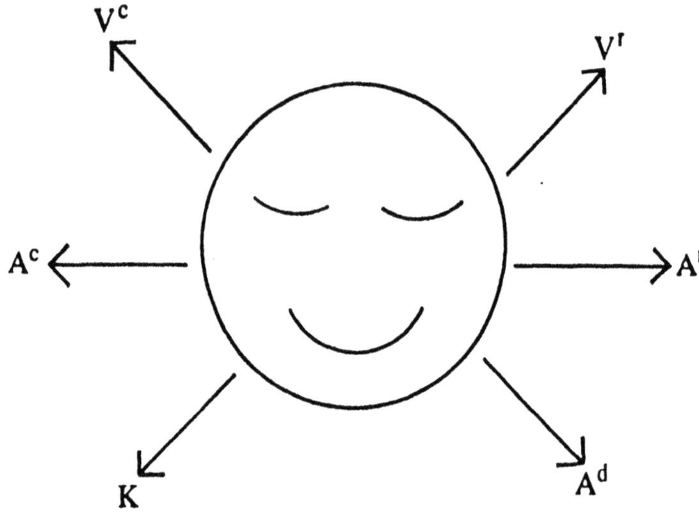

FIGURE 1

know." The counselor now has the following information: The client has scanned old alternatives (Vr), tried to make them applicable to new alternatives (Vc), failed and is feeling badly (K); furthermore the counselor knows that if he is going to present this client with options, he must allow the client to form pictures that he feels good about before this client can make a decision.

2. A female alcoholic explains that she may be unable to stay sober once she is back home. The counselor asks what might create a relapse. Right before the client answers, "My husband," he sees the woman's eyes move level to the left. Enriched with this information, he can now focus on the client's auditory representation of her husband, i.e., the tone of his voice, arguments, etc., as possible triggers for relapse. The session focuses on what is essential for this woman's sobriety, i.e., dealing with auditory triggers emanating from her husband which in the past had produced drinking responses.
3. A counselor discovers that there are times when an alcoholic client is able to refuse a drink and times when she "throws in the towel" and gets drunk. He carefully examines this process

with her and discovers the following in the client's decision making process. When she goes by her feelings (eyes in K), she drinks, but when she is able to take time out to discuss the issue with herself (eyes down to the left–internal dialogue), she generally can talk herself out of it. Counselor and client can now devise a strategy that enables the woman to move to Ad instead of K during risky times.

Of course, the examples are unlimited, but it is essential to introduce here the corollary of eye movements, the use of language. Individuals' internal representations of reality are echoes in their linguistic patterns, denoting primary visual, auditory and kinesthetic modes. Thus, an important NLP treatment tool is the ability to hear sensory based words, primarily the predicates. Dilts states: "A word only has meaning in the individualized primary sensory representations it triggers in the speaker or listener."[3] Some words clearly denote a client's visual propensity–"Now I see your point," others have an auditory focus "I hear what you are saying," and still a third group has a kinesthetic orientation, "I feel that I can do it." Of course, it is general knowledge that we, as therapists, are more successful when we speak our clients' language. One reason is that by speaking the client's language the resulting rapport increases significantly. Following are some examples of the use of linguistic patterns in the treatment of alcoholic clients.

1. An alcoholic client has made little progress and in group complains that he has been trying to focus on his recovery but cannot seem to get a perspective on his life. The counselor, noticing the visual predicates, asks him if he can picture his old pattern. When the client nods affirmatively, the counselor asks him to look more closely, so that he may get a clearer image of his present situation.
2. A counselor states to an alcoholic client: "Something tells me that you resent being here," and the client responds defensively, "I don't feel that way at all." If this discrepancy goes unnoticed, it may become a basis for a mismatch between counselor and client. It is useful for the counselor at a time like

this to "translate" his original statement to the level of kinesthetics, feelings, if he is to have a productive conversation with this client.

Use of language and eye patterns for obtaining information, establishing rapport and leading the interventions as quickly as possible in productive directions are some of the basic significant contributions Neuro-Linguistic Programming have made to the field of alcoholism treatment. Much of what was considered intuition or the famous "I don't know what worked, but something just clicked," pronouncements counselors make are actually reproducible skills, available at all times to a counselor. Furthermore, the more rapidly an effective intervention takes place, the more likely a client develops sufficient internal resources which will allow him to stay in treatment as well as sober. Effective and efficient calibrations and resulting interventions naturally speed up the treatment and recovery process. Replacing treatment's hit or miss approach with reliable information and techniques has a number of obviously significant benefits. In the first place, effective treatment moves a client toward well being more rapidly. Just as importantly, it being effective supports the alcoholism counselors in a field that has one of the highest rates of burnout of any profession. It is important for a counselor working with an alcoholic to feel confident in the use of his skills, in the knowledge that these skills are reliable. It is beneficial for the counselor and his mental health and it is an added benefit for the client, who frequently uses the counselor in early recovery as his model. Therefore, the content of the treatment as well as the context can make an effective contribution to the client's recovery.

For in-depth discussion of these two basic NLP themes, I would like to refer to the literature as extensively described in this monograph's bibliography.

ALCOHOLISM TREATMENT WITH NLP METHODOLOGY

NLP gives expanded ways of noticing important information that clients present to the therapist. This allows the therapist to make more efficient and effective interventions. Rather than obtaining knowledge for knowledge's sake, NLP is an action-oriented therapy, aimed at the process of moving clients as rapidly as is appropriate for them, toward well being. NLP is then a two-pronged approach to treatment. One, it increases awareness of the client's internal processes in measurable ways, and two, it provides very specific methodologies for the use of information obtained through clients' conscious and unconscious processes. The deliberateness of the treatment interventions has become a hallmark of Neuro-Linguistic Programming. This deliberateness then is connected to a high degree of flexibility in the approach to the alcoholic client. If the therapist's essential task with a client consists of adding choice to the alcoholic's repertoire, then flexibility geared at meeting the client in his model of the world is of primary importance. If internally no new choices are generated in the client, the organism will repeat – ad infinitum – choices that obviously no longer work in the present, but which at some point in time, appeared to have produced results. An NLP principle that was borrowed from its teachers, Milton Erickson, Fritz Perls, and Virginia Satir, is that people make the best choices they have available at any given time. People do not make bad choices, but are bound by internal limitations and make the best choices they have available internally under all circumstances. People make choices that are inappropriate because their map of the world does not contain the requisite options for more appropriate feelings and resulting behavior. Even though this process is described in different terminology within other human behavior systems, NLP works quite specifically with the concept of "Original Intent versus Manifested Behavior." Examples of this follow these patterns:

1. An alcoholic in early sobriety keeps missing appointments. Rather than labeling the behavior as resistance, the counselor examines this behavior carefully with the client and finds that arriving late is pervasive in the client's life on all levels, e.g., he misses enrollment at a local college by one day, does his taxes but forgets to mail them by April 15, etc. The client laughs sheepishly and calls himself a procrastinator. Careful investigation reveals that as a child, no matter what the client

produced, he was never good enough. Even if it was perfect, he was consistently criticized or downgraded for any achievement. The counselor uses a reframe that the alcoholic was a smart little kid to begin, at such an early age, to protect himself from adult onslaughts by simply not achieving or producing. The counselors asks the client if he was interested, now that he is an adult, in creating even more effective ways of dealing with inappropriate criticism. If the counselor had addressed the behavior of always coming late, the client would most likely have felt criticized, increasing the procrastinating behavior. By focusing on the original positive intent of the behavior, the counselor creates a frame for the client which shows lack of choice but functioning according to the client's ability, at the child's level. This allows the issue to become "increasing the client's internal repertoire of choices," leaving the value of the individual not only intact but actually increased.

2. In a group, an alcoholic client states that she only drinks when she is around people and that it never occurs to her to drink by herself. What becomes evident during further exploration is that the woman has a poor self-image which resulted in much shyness during the early teenage years. Needing to be liked, but having no skills in her repertoire to achieve this, she soon found alcohol, which decreased her inhibitions and made her outgoing, resulting initially in her increased popularity. Again, the counselor validates the original intent ("Of course people need people, that's what makes them human—you were clever enough to find a way to give to yourself what you needed"), separating it from the present behavior (alcohol abuse) and asking her if she is willing to explore additional, more effective ways of meeting her needs socially and dealing with her shyness.
3. A male alcoholic at the Salvation Army has all but destroyed every component of his earlier successful life but continues to drink heavily and thus puts himself at risk of being expelled from the program. Upon careful examination, the counselor finds a childhood of neglect, where the only way to obtain approval had been to go unnoticed. At age twelve he had

found a fairly permanent way of disappearing while remaining present, namely drinking alcoholically. Being expelled from the program would be just one more confirmation of people in authority's ability to make him disappear.

4. A young male client, addicted both to alcohol and cocaine is referred by his company's EAP with the following content in the referral note: "This client has been with 'D' company for five years and has worked his way to the top of his department three times. When he reaches the top, we—the company—don't see him for two weeks and then he comes back, remorseful, stating that he would get drunk." The young man turned out to be an abused child of an alcoholic mother and an absent father. The original positive intent of the behavior is reframed as an attempt at being independent, which eventually progressed to full-blown rebellion. Since both parents were unreliable at parenting, the client, out of self-preservation, had devised ways to function that were independent from his parents and chose to reject, out of distrust, any form of approval. Getting the high position at work took the place of this approval for his internal child. Even though the manifested behavior in the present, alcohol and cocaine abuse was inappropriate, the trigger, compliance (by reaching the top), was set off, creating old fears to which he continued to respond with "rebellion" or "independence," rejection of results which would leave him vulnerable to expectations of approval.

The above is reminiscent of a metaphor about old keys, something many of us do. I most certainly have a collection of old keys, as though one day, "they" will build me a lock to fit those keys, i.e., as though skills that were of the essence in making my life functional at some point, "ought" not to be obsolete at this time.

Positive Intent of Behavior versus the Manifested Behavior

Alcoholism as an illness may be held constant; the variable in the illness—why it starts when it does, and how it progresses—is an individual's unique contribution and needs to bear weight on the intervention if the treatment for alcoholism is going to be successful in the long run. Human beings experience the world through the screen of their individual experiences and these experiences qualify their perceptions. One of NLP's precepts is that all behavior makes sense in the context in which it was originated. Behavior, no matter how bizarre it may first appear to be, makes sense when it is perceived in the context of the choices generated by the individual's model of the world. The difficulty is not that the alcoholic is making a wrong choice but that he does not have sufficient internal choices—thus he acts on old instruction or generally outdated information that basically has no bearing on the present except that the present contains the trigger that sets the old behavior in motion. Thus, the client's internal representation of reality determines, to an important extent, this action, and not only his present reality itself. It is important to keep in mind that when the behavior was originally designed, it worked, at least better than anything else, and therefore became fixed. Thus, the important consideration in therapy becomes the creation of other ways of meeting the client's valid original objective. The stronger the behavior, the more likely it is initially connected to the client's survival issues, either by creating protection or nurturing and caring. The client's world has become impoverished and impoverished world concepts lead to limited choices.

A new NLP principle needs to be introduced at this time, the belief that given the opportunity, the organism naturally moves towards well being. Just as water flows along the path of the least resistance, so do people move in accordance with their healthy nature. Negative behavior or contrary behavior requires energy and the unconscious mind naturally selects the least costly form of operating. A small convincer exercise goes as follows: Close your eyes and internally identify a negative feeling of very limited importance. For this purpose, the feeling indeed has to be minor, like the one connected to forgetting one's keys or an irritation at a chore. Feel this minor negative feeling for a moment and give it sequentially a shape, size, color, temperature, and texture. Now change the shape, size, color, temperature, and texture and check internally what happened to the mild negative feeling. In most instances, this feeling has changed in a positive direction. People report a "lightening up," "disappearing," "movement to neutral," etc. The essential part of the exercise is that the instruction was "change" the elements, not "make it better." The organism indeed automatically moves toward well being, given the creation of internal choices. The problem is not that a client does not want to get better, but that internally new choices need to be generated if the alcoholic is to move toward recovery and well being.

Neuro-Linguistic Programming's primary goal is geared to generating internal choices for clients so that they may respond more competently to demands placed upon them by reality. Given a choice, people naturally choose well being over pain because this is the path of least resistance for the human organism. Thus, it is essential for the counselor to understand the alcoholic's "map" of the world and to be willing to join the client's internal representation of the world.

A final principle in the context of this chapter is NLP's presupposition that everything the client needs in his lifetime is already there in some form and that the treatment issue therefore becomes the way by which the client's internal resources can be accessed. Therapy has always been the process of bringing people to choice. NLP's contribution in this respect has been the design and creation of methodology that allows the client to access and employ these resources which will give him requisite variety. In other words, the purpose of discovering these resources is, in NLP language, to have a substantial "referential index," a repertoire of feelings and behaviors for the client to refer to which can appropriately take the place of drinking behavior. Examples may go as follows:

1. A recovering alcoholic gets angry when he is unjustly accused of neglecting his duties and "drinks at it." In tracing the behavior, he and the counselor find that accusations create an intense sense of being overwhelmed in the client. The work that follows focuses on creating internal options for identifying and then dealing with being overwhelmed.
2. A young woman has a slip after two years of sobriety and is devastated by the experience even though she is reassured about the occurrence and the meaning of the slip. In counseling it becomes obvious that for the first time during her sobriety she had taken a step toward improving her life situation and had enrolled at the local college. The relapse had protected

her from taking such a risk. The counseling process from that point was oriented at providing internal ways for this alcoholic client to protect herself and take care of herself even better than by drinking.

This last part, "even better" than the original negative past, is a corollary of the point under discussion which NLP explains as "never take choices away." The premise is that the organism will automatically choose an alternative that is the "least costly" to the human being, will automatically move toward well being. In alcoholism treatment, that means that the alcoholic will automatically choose sobriety instead of drinking, and that the only time non-sober behavior and subsequent alcoholic drinking occurs is when the organism lacks choice. Any choice is better than no choice and drinking behavior needs to remain part of the repertoire for an alcoholic in order to choose the alternative.

SUMMARY

NLP suppositions create a contextual framework rather than focus on the content of what transpires between counselor and client. The purpose and process of alcoholic behavior is the focus as opposed to why a person drinks excessively. The more choices are generated for the alcoholic both internally and in the counseling relationship, the better the chances are for continued sobriety. Regardless of the manifested behavior, NLP relies on the choice of the most positive behavior in a client available at a given time within the client's internal representation of reality.

Two basic skills that NLP brings to the field of treatment are calibration methods through the use of eye movements and specific ways of joining a client's model of the world with the use of the client's language on the process level in visual, auditory, and kinesthetic modes.

NLP's basic tenet is that the therapist can rely on the client's organism to naturally and automatically move towards well being and that the therapist's primary task is to create ways for clients to access their own internal resources.

REFERENCES

1. Bandler, R. and J. Grinder, *Frogs Into Princes*, p. IV.
2. Dilts, R., *Applications of Neuro-Linguistic Programming*, p. 9.
3. Ibid, p. 8.

Chapter 2

Neuro-Linguistic Programming: A Model for Behavioral Change in Alcohol and Other Drug Addiction

Eileen B. Isaacson, MSW, EdD, CAC

SUMMARY. This article describes the use of Neuro-Linguistic Programming (NLP) in working with clients who have been dependent on alcohol and other drugs. NLP is an approach to psychotherapy developed by Richard Bandler and John Grinder in the 1970s. The psycholinguistic systems model is designed to elicit information from the subjective representational sensory systems (visual, auditory, kinesthetic, olfactory and gustatory) and direct strategies to the conscious and unconscious processes of an individual for the purpose of facilitating behavioral change.

INTRODUCTION

Behavioral change in the area of alcohol/drug use is a complex task for the addicted individual and often requires assistance of professionals trained in chemical dependency. In an effort to address the problems of addiction, various theoretical models have been used to explain the addiction process including the medical/disease model, cognitive, sociocultural, psychological, social learning, etc. Although each model emphasizes a particular orientation to addiction, many theorists and practitioners would agree that knowledge of the drug, the individual and interactions with others and the environment are necessary in working with the addicted client (Brown, 1985; Kaufman & Kaufmann, 1979; Wegscheider-Cruse, 1985).

Brown (1985) suggests that addiction is characterized by behavioral and cognitive preoccupation with a substance and an overwhelming compulsion to have it. Mendelson and Mello (1985, p. 198) indicate that the syndrome of alcoholism has one constant feature: a significant life problem associated with the use of alcohol. Gallant (1987, p. 11) states "a drinking problem exists if the use of alcohol continues despite interference in any major area of a person's life: job or studies, relationships at home, social relationships, legal problems or medical complications." Marlatt and Rohsenow (1980) suggest that cognitive and environmental factors influence behaviors as strongly as the effect of a drug. They also identify the pressure of interpersonal conflict and social pressure as factors related to relapse.

The use of NLP in working with addictions is beginning to surface. Dilts (1983) suggests that habitual behavior is often a result of the person's least conscious representational system. NLP techniques are designed to work with the unconscious as well as the conscious. Andreas and Andreas (1987) have described techniques in working with alcohol and other drug compulsions as well as eating disorders. They have also described a technique called "Blowout" (1987, p. 96) as a way of ending an addictive relationship. Stanton Peele, MD (1975), an authority on addiction, has written on the addiction to an object relationship as well as alcohol or other drugs. Davis (1987) recommends the techniques of collapsing anchors and reframing, as strategies that have been successful in working with alcohol-related problems. Davis notes the importance of eliciting the function of the substance, which then serves as information in generating alternatives to the use of the addictive substance. Beletsis and Lovern (in Zeig, 1985) also suggest the use of hypnosis and techniques of NLP in working with alcohol addiction.

Working with clients who have alcohol and other drug problems necessitates assessing the process of addiction which is unique to that individual; this reinforces the need for professionals to be trained in the epistemology of addiction and to be skilled in eliciting information related to the individual's behavior in response to the drug, significant others, and the context of the environment. It is suggested that NLP is a model which can be utilized by therapists in working with clients to facilitate change in behaviors associated with addiction.

BACKGROUND

NLP was developed in the early 1970s by John Grinder and Richard Bandler. A model greatly influenced by Virginia Satir and Milton Erikson among others, NLP is a systems model which is directed to changing behavior by identifying existing patterns and intervening through sensory modes, verbally and non-verbally, in working with the conscious and unconscious processes of the client. It is the task of the therapist to work with the client in identifying problem behaviors and desired outcomes or goals in expanding the repertoire of available choices. In general, all therapies aim at changing behavior. In an effort to develop a framework for changing behavior using NLP, it is useful to understand some of the basic assumptions of the model which are as follows:

1. An individual has the resources necessary to make change.
2. An individual's communication is responsible for the response received in a communication.
3. Individuals experience internal and external events through sensory modes including visual, auditory, kinesthetic, olfactory and gustatory.
4. All behavior serves a purpose; behavior that is negative in terms of results is dependent of the value of the individual.
5. Behavior is to a great extent a function of unconscious motivation.
6. Change is made through addressing the ecology of the individual by working with the representational sensory modes.

As a model for therapy NLP provides a structure for therapists working with individuals. It can assist therapists to be more effective by identifying the client's favored representational system as a means to enhance communication and elicit information. Initial identification of the representational systems enables the therapist to match and pace the client verbally and non-verbally. Rapport, essential to all work between the client and therapist, is established through the strategy of matching and pacing (meeting the client verbally in the same sensory mode, e.g., if visual, the client might use such predicates as I see what you mean, or I get the picture, the image of . . . etc.), and non-verbally (the therapist matching body language, using tone of voice, i.e., volume, rate of talking, etc.). Once rapport is established the therapist can lead the client into other representational modes to expand the client's experience and choices. According to Bandler and Grinder (1979, p. 17) "You will always get answers to your questions insofar as you have the sensory apparatus to notice the responses."

To elicit information effectively, Bandler and Grinder suggest that the therapist must be in "up-time," i.e., completely in sensory experience with the client, exclusive of the therapist's own internal feelings, visualizations or sounds. This requires complete attention focused by the therapist on observing how the client is responding. This provides a general framework for the use of NLP. The next section presents definitions of addiction and some of the major elements of the model. These will assist in working toward an integration of NLP as a tool for working with alcohol and other drug addiction.

DEFINITIONS

Psychoactive Substance Addiction/ Dependence and Substance Abuse

Addiction is used interchangeably in this paper in reference to alcohol and other psychoactive (mood altering) drugs. The DSM III-R (1987, p. 166) definition of psychoactive substance dependence is presented as: A cluster of "cognitive, behavioral and physiologic symptoms" that indicate the person has impaired control over psychoactive use and continues use of the substance despite adverse consequences. Symptoms include physical tolerance and withdrawal.

Substance Abuse as differentiated from dependence in the DSM III-R (1987, p. 169) is defined as "a maladaptive pattern of psychoactive substance use" and does not include physical withdrawal. The cases described in this paper were all characterized by abuse and dependence at some point in their use of psychoactive substances.

It should be noted that addiction extends beyond the use of alcohol and other drugs and may include eating disorders, gambling and addiction to a relationship. For the purposes of this paper addiction will focus on the use of psychoactive substances.

Neuro-Linguistic Programming. A model of the structure of an individual's subjective experience and how that experience influences behavior. As a model it provides a framework for eliciting the way individuals experience reality with a focus on reorganizing the way individuals experience and respond to their own models of the world (Dilts, 1976, p. 14).

Meta-Model. A representation, of the grammatical representation of an individual's experience, used to obtain information regarding perceptions of experience. Experience which individuals have can differ from reality in 3 ways: experience will contain deletions, distortions, and generalizations. For a detailed description of the model the reader is referred to Bandler and Grinder's work in *The Structure of Magic* (1975).

Representational System. The sensory processing system that initiates and modulates behavior; the system consists of visual, auditory, kinesthetic, gustatory and olfactory senses (Lankton, 1980, p. 16).

Anchor. A trigger or stimulus which elicits a memory response and behavior. The therapist may anchor a desired outcome response through use of a sensory mode, i.e., visual, auditory, or kinesthetic. For example, pressure on the wrist might be used to "anchor" a pleasant experience that has been elicited using all representational systems. Thus touching the wrist would evoke the pleasant memory.

Submodalities. Internal and external representations of sensory modes used to elicit information in moving toward a desired outcome. Examples of submodalities within the sensory modes include:

> Visual: color, shape, size, distance, shape
> Auditory: tone, sound, volume, pitch, tempo
> Kinesthetic: pressure, intensity, weight, pulse, temperature
> Olfactory, Gustatory: bitter, sweet, salty, sour

Pacing. A means of establishing rapport by using body posture, gestures, tone of voice, rate of breathing, rate of speed to match the client.

Reframing. Process of creating "a framework in which all parts of the system are aligned toward achieving the desired outcome" (Dilts et al., 1980). Anchors are used to (1) evoke the problem behavior, (2) evoke the desirable behavior and (3) elicit the desirable behavior by collapsing the anchors. A Six-Step Reframe Summary, adapted from Bandler and Grinder (1975) is provided in Figure 2.1.

Future Pacing. Process of connecting the new response with the relevant context for change (Bandler & Grinder, 1979) using all

Figure 2.1. Six-Step Reframe Summary

1. Identify the pattern to be changed.
2. Establish communication with the part responsible for the pattern. Once established, use representational systems and submodalities to work with changing the pattern.
3. Determine the function of the pattern and separate the pattern from the positive function (assumption: all behaviors serve some positive function, e.g., drinking functions to allow an individual to be more outgoing, social).
4. Access a creative part and generate new behaviors to accomplish the positive function.
5. Future Pace by asking the creative part if it is willing to take responsibility for using new alternative behaviors when it seems appropriate.
6. Ecological Check by asking if any part of the client objects to using the new alternative behaviors. If the response is "yes," go back to Step 2.

(The writer of this paper has found that in some cases going back to Step 4 may also work.)

representational sensory modes to reinforce the change. This will tell you if it is consistent with the ecological state of the individual. If it is not, then another reframe will be necessary.

Ecological State of the Client. This represents the comfortability of the client with the new alternatives for change. In questioning the client, the therapist will be able to determine whether the change will be implemented.

Imbedded Commands. A command statement to promote the desired outcome inserted in the dialogue by the therapist.

Conscious. "Whatever you are aware of at a moment in time" (Bandler and Grinder, 1979, p. 37).

> *NLP: Implementing the Model for Change.* In coming to understand how people continue to cause themselves pain and dissatisfaction, it is important to realize that they are not bad. They are in fact making the best choices that they are aware of; that is the best choice available in their model of the world. In other words, human beings; behavior, no matter how bizarre it may seem, will make sense when it is viewed in the context of the choices generated by their models.

The foregoing words of Bandler and Grinder (1979, p. 77) are basic to understanding individual behavior. Accepting the premise that an individual's behavior is a function of how she/he is experiencing internal and external stimuli both consciously and unconsciously has implications for the therapist in utilizing techniques of NLP.

NLP as a systems model for change is presented in Figure 2.2. The therapist uses the meta-model to elicit information through all stages in working with problems behavior and moving toward desired outcome or goal. The model depicts four stages: I. Eliciting Information; II. Application of Strategies for Change; III. Behavioral Outcome; and IV. Feedback to the Therapist.

Stage I

This stage includes (a) establishing rapport by pacing, through the use of matching breathing rate, representational systems, tone of voice, etc., (b) obtaining information about the problem behav-

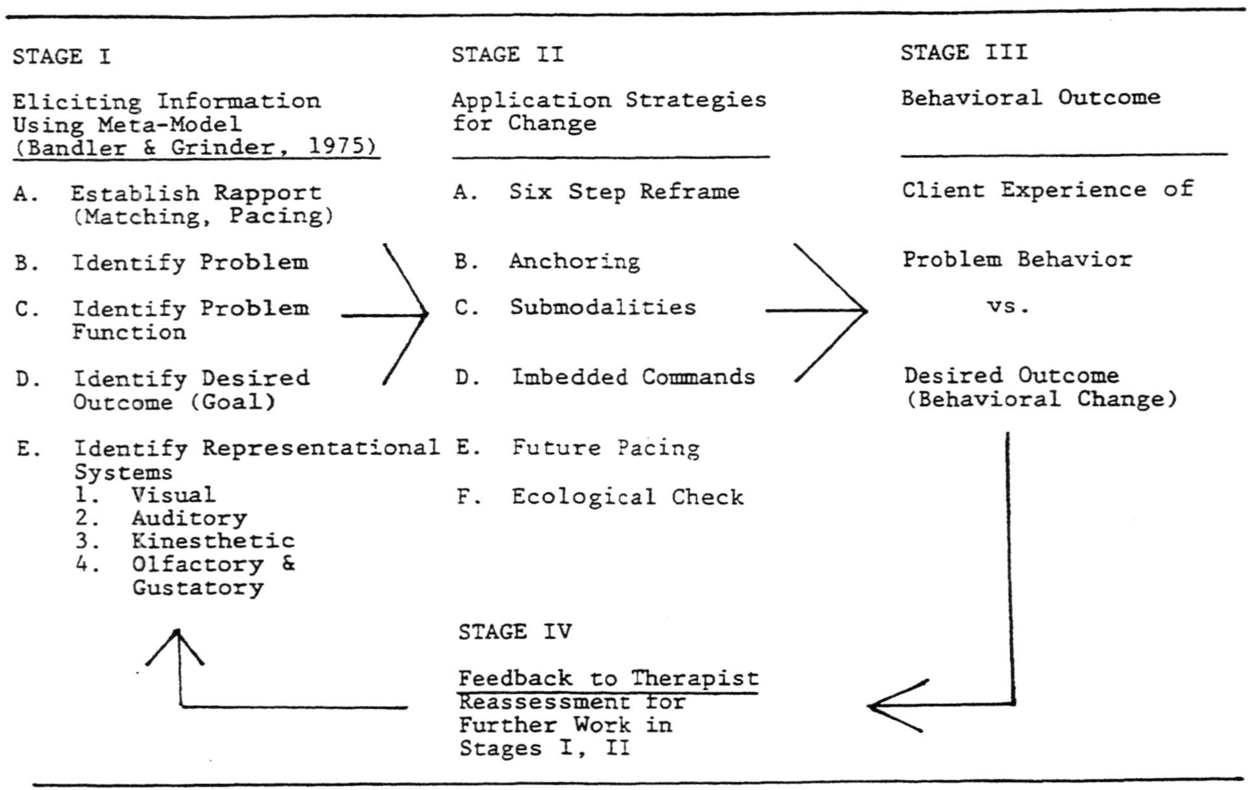
STAGE I
Eliciting Information Using Meta-Model (Bandler & Grinder, 1975)
A. Establish Rapport (Matching, Pacing)
B. Identify Problem
C. Identify Problem Function
D. Identify Desired Outcome (Goal)
E. Identify Representational Systems
1. Visual
2. Auditory
3. Kinesthetic
4. Olfactory & Gustatory
STAGE II
Application Strategies for Change
A. Six Step Reframe
B. Anchoring
C. Submodalities
D. Imbedded Commands
E. Future Pacing
F. Ecological Check
STAGE III
Behavioral Outcome
Client Experience of
Problem Behavior
vs.
Desired Outcome (Behavioral Change)
STAGE IV
Feedback to Therapist
Reassessment for Further Work in Stages I, II

FIGURE 2.2

iors, (c) the functions served, (d) identifying the desired outcome or goal, and (e) utilizing the client's representational systems to identify limiting patterns of behavior and develop new resources to facilitate desired outcome behaviors.

Stage II

Based on the information elicited in Stage I, strategies are selected to expand client's options for behavioral change. Strategies used in the case application include (a) reframing, (b) anchoring, (c) use of submodalities, (d) imbedded commands, (e) future pacing (used to check the applicability of the new behaviors to the client's environment during the session), and (f) checking client's ecological state.

Stage III

The success of the expanded behavioral options is reported by the client as situations are tested.

Stage IV

Feedback to the therapist regarding the success or failure of the client's experience provides information for further work. The next section describes the process application of the model to cases involving addiction.

CASE APPLICATION

The cases identified describe the application of the Six-Step Reframe (Figure 2.1) (Bandler & Grinder, 1982, pp. 114-115) in working with a male having a primary diagnosis of alcoholism, a female who was dually diagnosed with a primary diagnosis of depression and a secondary diagnosis of alcoholism, and a male with polydrug history including heroin, cocaine and alcohol dependence. The NLP Systems Model (Figure 2.2) is useful in depicting the stages of work. It is important to note that as an integrated systems model, the therapist used the meta-model, and sensory representational systems throughout each stage of the process in order to elicit information and maintain rapport. Although the therapist used future pacing and checked the client's ecological state, the success of the work is reality tested when the client is back in his/her environment. Thus, feedback after the session(s) is necessary to determine what additional work, if any, is necessary. The number of sessions required varies with the client, therapist and the work to be done.

CASE 1

Background

The client is a 26-year-old male whose primary abuse had been alcohol. He was 3 months abstinent and finding it increasingly difficult to attend Alcoholics Anonymous (AA) meetings with an increasing desire to drink.

The client identified an "increasing craving for alcohol" as the problem. He wanted to eliminate the desire to drink. In using the meta-model, it was noted that the client's primary representational system was kinesthetic. He found himself almost tasting the "smoothness" of whiskey in his mouth. This was happening to him on a daily basis after work and he found himself taking a route home that was close to the bar he had frequented when drinking. His social life had revolved almost exclusively with drinking friends.

Six-Step Reframe

In doing a Six-Step Reframe the following sequence occurred:

1. The problem was identified as "I'm scared, I want to be sober, but there's a part of me that wants to drink."

   Desired Outcome: *"I want to be sober."*

2. Eliciting the part that wanted to drink, it was found that the desire for alcohol was supported by the client's *representational systems* as described below. Asking the client to changes submodalities of the sensory representations affected the desire for alcohol and was useful in giving the client choices when he would feel the urge to drink.

Representations Supporting Drinking	Representations Facilitating Change
• feeling the smooth, warm, texture of the imagined alcohol	• diluting the liquid, lowering the temperature
• hearing sounds of laughter of bar friends and music	• lowering volume of laughter, music
• seeing the wood stools in earth tones, red-orange lights	• changing color of the barroom to gray, bright white lighting
• smell of malt and beer	• making the smell sharp (ammonia)

3. The client was directed to ask the part that supported drinking, what *function the drinking served*. It was elicited that drinking helped the client to feel comfortable in social situations and reduce the anxiety of talking with people. The part was also asked if it would be willing to try out other behaviors that would do what the alcohol had done. The part agreed.
4. The client was asked to *access a creative part* to generate at least three alternatives to drinking. Signals were given as each was identified.
5. In an effort to *future pace*, the client was asked to find out if the creative part would take responsibility for using the alternatives generated. The part agreed.
6. The client was asked if any of the parts objected to the new behavior changes. There was no apparent disagreement. It appeared that the *ecological system* of the client was supported.

Imbedded Command Technique

One of the difficulties the client had been having was to find a sponsor. At the end of the session an imbedded command was given by the therapist, "You may be surprised that you will find a sponsor very soon and it will be your choice."

Outcome

The client reported finding a sponsor within the following two weeks. Follow-up sessions included checking out what the client was experiencing in an effort to obtain feedback regarding the choices available in maintaining change. It was necessary to go back and reinforce options available when the kinesthetic representations supporting drinking surfaced again. It should be noted that the strongest representational system of the client is often the one needing more work. The client maintained sobriety for six months when he was transferred to a job out of state and terminated treatment.

CASE 2

Background

The client is a 45-year-old female (Mrs. J) who had a primary diagnosis of depression and secondary diagnosis of alcoholism. She had been treated for alcoholism at age 40 and was on mood elevators.

Problem Identification

The presenting problems identified by the client were: (1) "I feel as though I have no control over my life, and I'm worried about drinking again." (2) "I am having trouble with my husband and am thinking of getting a divorce."

When eliciting substance abuse history the client said she felt like drinking when she argued with her husband and on two occasions did. The therapist discussed the danger of drinking and taking prescription medication. The client was encouraged to speak with the physician who had prescribed the drug; a release was also signed so the therapist could contact the physician.

Problem 1: "I'm worried about drinking."

Desired Outcome Identified by the Client

"The first thing I want is not to drink." (A conscious agreement was made not to drink and to attend AA meetings during the time of therapy.)

In sessions with Mrs. J, a pattern of events occurred leading up to her drinking. She would feel a pain in her stomach and feel lonely and depressed. (This occurred when she was waiting for her husband to come home.) She would see herself alone and abandoned and experience silence as she had when her parents divorced when she was 7 years old.

Six-Step Reframe

A Six-Step Reframe was done to elicit some alternative behaviors when she would feel lonely and angry. The result was that she became involved in outside activities including joining a church group and doing volunteer work. These new activities took the place of being angry and waiting for Mr. J to meet her expectations. The drinking did not recur although the client did not continue AA meetings regularly. Mr. J started to come home more often as Mrs. J was more involved in outside activities.

Problem 2: Eliciting Information/Representational Sensory Modes

Both the client and Mr. J were seen at this point. During three sessions it was noted that Mr. J's favored representational system was identified as visual: "I can't see that what she (client) says makes any sense. I come home more than I did. Things would be fine if she would let me alone."

Problem Identification

(Mrs. J's representational system was Kinesthetic.)

"We haven't been intimate . . . you (to Mr. J) haven't touched me in months."

Desired Outcome: Mrs. J

When asked what she wanted, the client said she wanted Mr. J to spend time with her . . . "the way we used to." He doesn't pay any attention to me—when we go out with friends he dances with other women but not with me."

The following intervention was made with Mr. J.

Desired Outcome: Checking with Mr. J

Therapist: Mr. J it seems difficult for you to see what Mrs. J is feeling and she is saying she would like to be closer with you. I'm wondering if there are times when you can see yourself close with her? . . . intimate? . . .

Mr. J: Responds yes to both inquiries.

Anchoring Desired Outcome

Therapist: Can you picture a time you were close and enjoyed being with her? (The expression on his face softened and he nodded. At that moment the therapist pressed his wrist to anchor the visual and kinesthetic representations.)

Therapist: I'd like to ask you to picture the scene again. Can you see if there are any sounds in the picture?

Mr. J: Yes, there's music.

Therapist: Can you identify how it sounds?

Mr. J: No, just soft music—string instruments probably, they're my favorite.

Therapist: Can you feel the scene once more and hear the music? (Therapist presses his wrist once again in response to his facial cues.)

Therapist: To Mr. J and Mrs. J: It seems that there's a pattern leading up to your arguments. Mrs. J, when your expectations aren't met, and Mr. J doesn't come home, you get angry. Then Mr. J gets angry and distances. I'd like to ask if you'd be willing to try something. (Looks at both Mr. and Mrs. J; they agree.) Mrs. J when you want to express a need to be with Mr. J, I'm going to ask you not to say anything but just go over and put your hand on Mr. J's wrist . . . like this. Is that all right with both of you? Both agreed.

Outcome

Mrs. J reported that Mr. J was spending more time with her and they had been intimate on one occasion over the weeks between this and the following session. Mrs. J was involved in outside activities, did not drink until the time of termination, a total of 3 months.

CASE 3

Background

The client is a 32-year-old male with a 15-year history of heroin, cocaine and alcohol dependence. He had completed short term in-residence treatment 3 times. He was married to a drug user; they have been divorced 6 months.

Problem Identification

The presenting problem as identified by the client was: "I have a problem in relationship with females. It seems I always pick some-one and give my blood and guts to it. Then I get hurt when a girl doesn't respond the same way."

Desired Outcome by the Client

"I don't want to get hooked and wind up hurt. I do the same thing over and over. I want to stop."

The favored representational sensory system of the client is kinesthetic—"I feel it in my gut."

Six-Step Reframe

The Six-Step Reframe was used to elicit information from the client to establish the sequence of events in the patterns of behavior, identify submodalities within the representational systems, identify the part that supported the unwanted behavior, identify the creative part to generate alternative behaviors, future pace, and check the client's ecological system.

Eliciting information regarding patterns, representational systems and submodalities follows.

Client: I find myself thinking about a girl (it's always the same with every girl). I have to be with her all the time. It's just like I felt when I needed cocaine or heroin – it's just like a drug.

Therapist: How does it start?

Client: First I find myself thinking about her (looks up to the left; client is in visual mode – recreating an image).

Therapist: What happens if you bring the image closer?

Client: I want to touch her and be with her.

Therapist: What color is the picture?

Client: Bright red.

Therapist: What happens if you make it blue? Does it make you want to be with her more or less?

Client: Less.

Therapist: If you move it away from you does it get less or more intense?

Client: Less.

Therapist: What happens if you make it smaller?

Client: I don't feel the pull as strongly.

Therapist: Are there sounds?

Client: No, wait there's something like a beat . . . getting louder like heavy metal.

Therapist: What happens if you make it louder?

Client: It really pulls me in. I want to be with her more.

Therapist: What happens if you lower the volume?

Client: The feeling gets less intense.

Therapist: Try changing the music to violin . . . what happens?

Client: I can't stand violin music. I want to push it away.

Therapist: Now try making the picture blue, pushing it far in front of you, and take out the music. Does it make you want to be there more or less?

Client: Less.
Therapist: I'd like you to make a movie of the whole scene and turn it slowly so that you see each frame pass by. What happens?
Client: I'm finding myself pulled in and wanting to be there more.
Therapist: Make it in color.
Client: I want it more.
Therapist: Speed up the pictures. How is it now?
Client: I don't feel as much of a pull.
Therapist: Speed it up and make it black and white. How is it now?
Client: Too fast for me to catch up with.
Therapist: Speed it up more, keep it black and white, take away the sound. How is it now?
Client: It doesn't get me at all.
Therapist: Make it smaller, and move it farther away. Now how is it?
Client: Almost gone. I don't get any feeling.
Therapist: Now make it bigger, and bring it closer. How is it now?
Client: I'm feeling myself pulled in again.
Therapist: Make it smaller, keep it black and white, speed it up until it goes faster and faster and keeps moving away. How is it now?
Client: I can barely see it. It's moving so fast, it's gone.
Therapist: How is it for you now?
Client: I feel as though something is missing.
Therapist: Bring the movie back and move it closer to you, slow it down, keep it black and white, slow music at low volume. How is it now?
Client: It's nothing. I can take it or leave it.
Therapist: Be aware that you can use these strategies of changing size, shape, color, sound, etc., to work in helping you change your experience and behavior.

Identifying Function of the Compulsive Behavior

Therapist: Ask the part of you that supports the compulsive behavior what function it serves.

Client: I don't have to be all alone, I always know someone is there for me and only me. I feel secure and comfortable.

Therapist: Ask that part of you if it would be willing to consider letting other things take the place of the addiction to any person or thing?

Client: It's willing to give it a try.

Identifying Alternative Behaviors

Therapist: Now I'm going to ask you to go inside yourself and ask a creative part of you to help identify some alternatives to focusing on one object.

Client: O.K.

Therapist: Is that part willing?

Client: Nods yes.

Therapist: Checks out the nod; reaffirmed.

Future Pacing

Therapist: Ask the creative part of you to start generating alternative behaviors that can be resources to you and provide options when you are feeling compelled by a relationship. Have that part identify as many as possible and let me know by signaling me with your index finger each time. (Observes the client while the process works – 6 alternatives observed.)

Therapist: I'd like to ask that part to take responsibility for generating alternatives as appropriate to assist you in developing new behaviors. Please ask if it is willing and signal . . . (nods).

First Ecological Check

Therapist: Is there any part that is unwilling to allow new choices to be generated?
Client: There's a part still concerned about a void that may be left.
Therapist: Goes back to check the part supporting the problem behavior and then to the creative part to generate more alternatives.

Second Ecological Check

Lets therapist know that all parts are willing to have choices generated.

Outcome

At the next session the client reported feeling compelled to be with the female in question. He decided to stay with the feeling and time framed it allowing himself to be with it for 30 minutes. He made it through 20 minutes and then went to an N.A. meeting. (NA stands for Narcotics Anonymous, a twelve step self-help recovery program for drug dependent or addicted individuals.) He planned to build in other activities—playing cards on one night with friends and going to a party with friends free of drug use. It is useful to note that when the same alternatives were discussed earlier utilizing one representational mode and conscious process, they were not utilized by the client.

The use of NLP as a tool for behavior change in alcohol and other drug addiction is beginning to surface. The primary value of the model is that it facilitates change by working systematically with the conscious and unconscious representations of an individual.

Specifically applied to chemically dependent clients it can be effective in working to change rigid thinking and behavior patterns characteristic of this population. Such patterns include dealing with denial and rationalization among other defense mechanisms which support denial and rationalization among other defense mechanisms which support rigidity. The focus on patterns related to addiction is accomplished by using the model in moving the client toward developing and expanding options in maintaining abstinence and sobriety.

The NLP framework for effecting behavioral change and increased options includes establishing rapport, using the meta-model for eliciting information, identifying favored representational sensory modes (visual, auditory, kinesthetic, olfactory and gustatory) and expanding the use of these systems for increased alternatives. These elements for NLP, as well as the specific strategies of Six-Step Reframe, anchoring, and the use of imbedded commands are used as interventions in the cases presented in this paper. The application of the strategies is described in work with three clients—an alcohol dependent male, a male polydrug user, and a female who was dually diagnosed (primary diagnosis of depression with a secondary diagnosis of alcoholism).

In sum, the effectiveness of NLP in working with the chemically dependent client, is a function of the therapist's, (1) knowledge of NLP as well as chemical addiction and (2) skill in applying the elements of the model in working with problems and desired outcomes identified by the client. The use of NLP is strongly recommended to therapists in working with chemically dependent clients.

REFERENCES

Andreas, S., & Andreas, C. (1987). *Change your mind and keep the change.* Moab, Utah: Real People Press.

American Psychiatric Association. (1987). *DSM III-R.* Washington, DC.

Bandler, R., & Grinder, J. (1975). *The structure of magic.* Palo Alto, CA: Science and Behavior Books.

Bandler, R., & Grinder, J. (1982). *Reframing neuro-linguistic programming and the transformation of meaning.* Moab, Utah: Real People Press.

Bandler, R., & Grinder, J. (1985). *Using your brain for change. Neuro-linguistic programming.* Moab, Utah: Real People Press.

Beletsis, C. (1985). An Eriksonian approach in the treatment of alcoholism. In J. K. Zeig, *Eriksonian psychotherapy. Vol. II. Clinical applications.* New York: Brunner/Mazel, Inc.

Brown, S. (1985). *Treating the alcoholic: A developmental model of recovery.* New York: John Wiley and Sons.

Davis, D., MD (1987). *Alcoholism treatment. An integrative family and individual approach.* New York: Gardner Press, Inc.

Dilts, R. B. (1983). *Part I: Roots of neuro-linguistic programming.* Cupertino, CA: Meta Publications.

Dilts, R. B., Grinder, J., Bandler, R., Bandler, L. C., & DeLozier, J. (1980). *Neuro-linguistic programming: Vol. I. The study of subjective experience.* Cupertino, CA: Meta Publications.
Gallant, D. M. (1987). *Alcoholism. A guide to diagnosis, intervention and treatment.* New York: W. W. Norton & Co., Inc.
Kaufman, E., & Kaufmann, P. (1979). *Family therapy of drug and alcohol abuse.* New York: Gardner Press, Inc.
Lankton, S. (1980). *Practical magic: A translation of basic neuro-linguistic programming into clinical psychotherapy.*
Lovern, J. D. (1985). Unconscious factors in recovery from alcoholism: The James-Jung Erikson connection. In J. K. Zeig, *Eriksonian psychotherapy. Vol. II. Clinical applications.* New York: Brunner/Mazel, Inc.
Marlatt, G. A., & Gordon, J. R. (Eds.). (1985). *Relapse prevention. Maintenance strategies in the treatment of addictive behaviors.* New York: The Guilford Press.
Marlatt, G. A., & Rohsenow, D. J. (1980). Cognitive processes in alcohol use. Expectancy and the balanced placebo design. In N. K. Mello (Ed.), *Advances in substance abuse* (Vol. I). Greenwich, CT: JAI Press.
Wegscheider-Cruse. (1985). *Another chance.* Palo Alto, CA: Science and Behavior Books.
Zeig, J. K. (1985). *Eriksonian psychotherapy. Vol. II. Clinical applications.* New York: Brunner/Mazel, Inc.

Chapter 3

Neuro-Linguistic Programming Rapport Skills and Alcoholism Treatment

Chelly M. Sterman, MSW, ABECSW, CAC

INTRODUCTION

All therapists consciously or unconsciously use an arsenal of rapport skills, a set of patterns that allows them to create a working relationship with clients in a most expedient way. Creating rapport is part of an intervention and conversely, the chances of success of an intervention increase in part in accordance with the quality of rapport created prior to the intervention. Frequently, an alcoholic client will say, "I really did not want to do it, but I knew he (the counselor) was doing his best for me, had been right in the past, seemed like he really cared, etc." Then the client will take a risk that previously had not been part of his internal repertoire. The motivation will at least partly be fueled by the strength of the rapport between client and counselor.

Often timing is essential in alcoholism treatment. In order to achieve maximum success as rapidly as possible in the relationship with an alcoholic client and those who belong to his alcoholic system effective and efficient rapport skills are the quickest way of what in an earlier chapter was called "Joining your client's model of the world." In addition, a second part will be explored here which may be formulated as: After you join your client's model of the world, you then need to lead him to his internal resources so that his model of the world can be sufficiently enlarged to move him toward sobriety and general well being. Denial and resistance, the Latin words "denego" and "resista" meaning literally "intensely saying no" and "withstanding," are skills the alcoholic employs that allow him to remain "safely" in his addiction until such time that conditions are created that invite him into sobriety. Competent rapport skills can create such an invitation and it frequently is the easiest and most comfortable, least demanding invitation to sobriety. Once the alcoholic experiences being met in his world by a powerful modeler, his counselor, he can also experience a more extensive self. The increased internal safety—his own now coupled with the therapist's—allows for testing new choices which are better suited for his survival than drinking alcoholically. The most significant model for this appears in Alcoholics Anonymous (AA) meetings which form a strong rapport and modeling framework. The alcoholic in early sobriety is accepted without demands being placed upon him, older members introduce themselves and through modeling and very specific teaching (the steps, traditions, and a whole set of rules and beliefs about quality recovery) lead him to safety. These are the two skills Neuro-Linguistic Programing (NLP) has studied extensively in the formation of rapport. They are called "pacing" and "leading" and NLP's contribution is to make these skills teachable by examining their components and by creating skills for duplicating these components.

BASIS FOR CREATING RAPPORT

Yeager defines the structure of rapport as:

> The establishment of a cooperative communication mode where harmony, trust, and positive emotional responses characterize the dialogue. This is often achieved by pacing or matching aspects of the other person's non-verbal body language which generates positive kinesthetic responses . . . [1]

Cameron in describing the methods for achieving rapport states:

> Your client will experience the interaction as a high context communication while allowing you to gather the needed information graciously in order to make your map of their experience an accurate one.[2]

Cameron further describes mirroring or pacing as a specific pattern of "offering back to the client portions of their nonverbal behavior—just as a mirror does."[3] Pacing or mirroring is as natural as tapping your foot to the sound of some engaging music. Much mirroring is done automatically, especially on a larger scale. People tend to behave fairly congruently in groups in any situations. For instance, a barroom brawl that becomes a free for all is based on this mirroring principle. People en masse get into fights, not because they have a stake in any particular issue, but because they get into rapport with the other fighters. Or, when someone in a group brings in a cake and starts singing "Happy Birthday," virtually everybody will join in, laugh, and clap even before finding out what the occasion is, again an example of rapport being an automatic occurrence. What NLP has done is taken this automatic occurrence and made it teachable as specific skills in the context of counseling. According to Cameron, "Mirroring is . . . a way to imitate the high context messages the client is giving without attaching meaning to them."[4]

ELEMENTS OF RAPPORT SKILLS

Visual, auditory, and kinesthetic awareness are the added tools NLP brings to alcoholism treatment in regard to rapport skills. In order for the alcoholic client to understand what the therapist is saying, he has to take the therapist's words—which are in essence arbitrary labels for part of the therapist's personal history—and access his own meaning for these words, that which corresponds with his own meaning. NLP describes the latter activity as a form of a transderivational search.

To present an example, an alcoholic in treatment states:

"Women have destroyed my trust and that is why I drink." The therapist has a number of choices at that time. NLP chooses some specific ones. When using NLP methodology, the counselor asks three questions: (1) "All women?" or "Who specifically has destroyed your trust?" (Mother? First girl friend?), (2) "What specifically do you mean by destroyed? (Is it totally gone, always?), and (3) "What does trust mean to you?" (Will women steal your money, want too much from you, abandon you?). A counselor who does not gather this information will be less capable of joining the client's model of the world and pace the alcoholic appropriately because what he will pace is his own representation of women, destroy, and trust. Pacing and leading, the two elements of rapport skills encompass the various forms of rapport counselors already successfully use and some less familiar ones as well. To restate, the purpose of the use of these skills is the creation of an effective base for therapist-client communication, a sense of alliance with the client which in turn broadens his basis from which to grow, from which to risk facing life without the use of alcohol or other drugs. As AA has taught, one of the most effective ways for an alcoholic to go into recovery is to be consistently able to borrow from someone else's strength (higher power, the group, sponsor). The emphasis on this format of communication is important in all therapist-client relationships but is especially true for alcoholics who, generally for a considerable period of time, have relied on an external resource, alcohol, for their continuation of life or survival. The alcoholic, therefore, has excellent prior rapport skill training since he has been geared toward consistently borrow strength externally. The therapist or the AA group are likely to be some of the first people he can borrow from in healthy ways, in ways that develop choice. Thus, excellent rapport creates the invitation to move toward sobriety.

NLP has developed this invitation in the form of rapport skills and what follows is a description of these rapport skills as they apply to alcoholism treatment.

What is it that allows one counselor to create immediate rapport with a client and this rapport, for another counselor, remain illusive or laborious? How specifically do you measure rapport in alcoholism treatment? NLP does not believe in the mere "readiness" in clients—it makes itself actively responsible for the client's readiness by using a vast repertoire of techniques, some of which will be explored in a later chapter. The ones focused on in this chapter are the pacing and leading skills, the rapport between counselor and client.

PACING

Each therapist who runs a group is aware of the following: When a group has been sitting very quietly, and one person shifts position, many of the group members switch position, frequently in a similar fashion. Or, in individual sessions, when an alcoholic client is very depressed, the therapist may have a tendency to slow down and flatten out his own voice. Both are examples of specific rapport skills, the first one on a visual and kinesthetic level, the second one on an auditory level.

What exactly is meant by pacing? Yeager states that:

> This involves observing the client, eliciting information, and selecting one or more aspects of the clients' body language. You then adjust your own body language to match those aspects of the client. In the majority of (therapeutic) situations this matching will occur spontaneously. It is only necessary to consciously select pacing tools if you sense that there is something missing from the dialogue.[5]

Generally, there is a combination of the following rapport components that make up the pacing skills whether they occur naturally or whether they are used consciously by the therapist. The rapport components correspond to the visual, auditory, and kinesthetic element of human functioning described elsewhere in this monograph. Thus, mirroring on its various levels is the behavioral equivalent of accepting the client verbally. Portions of the client's behavior that present themselves for the purpose of mirroring include body postures, specific gestures, facial expressions, voice tone, tempo, and intonation patterns and breathing rhythms. Matching some of these (all are rarely necessary and especially in the beginning would draw too much conscious attention away from the counselor's interaction with the client) will assist the therapist in achieving a harmonious interaction: "In fact by mirroring it is possible to disagree with the content portion of a person's communication and remain in complete rapport."[6] The more the therapist practices the more aware he may become of the rhythms he and his clients generate with gestures and breathing patterns and in voice tones, tempo, rhythms, etc. It is especially fascinating to observe couples who come for counseling in early sobriety and to see how out of sync they generally are. As the marital therapy progresses, the therapist can observe more congruity between the partners. If this congruity does not appear, it may be wise to double check clients' assertions that "We are doing much better." To reiterate, the most significant pacing or mirroring elements available to the therapist consist of (1) V: posture, gestures, facial expression, (2) A: rate, tone, rhythm, pitch, intonation of speech, and (3) K: breathing rate.

The following vignette may serve as an example. A woman, sober two years, goes to meetings regularly, but on occasion smokes pot and does not see anything wrong with it. Her sponsor suggests that she see a therapist. After the therapist establishes rapport, he does a verbal confrontation, maintaining rapport on a visual level. Rapport is maintained in spite of the client's anger and defensiveness and the alcoholic, feeling accepted and understood, can free up enough internal energy to give up denisto – denial (vigorously saying no) – and examine her behavior.

It is important to emphasize that this process involves mirroring, not mimicking. The pacing skills are not to be perceived as a parody of the client, but as a harmonious joining so that the client knows that the therapist is willing to meet him in his model of the world, be his ally before the alcoholic is requested to change. Resistance to change is a natural side product of insufficient rapport. Conversely, changework is likely to be most successful when rapport is created and maintained. Therefore, it is essential for the therapist during the course of an intervention to frequently check for rapport, and go back to step one, establishment of rapport, if he finds that for any reason rapport was interrupted.

The following case is presented as a demonstration. A client was referred by the Bureau for Motor Vehicles after he was stopped during a routine maneuver by local police. A certain amount of alcohol was found in his blood and he had to complete an eight week educational course at which time he was requested to fill out a questionnaire regarding alcohol use. The results of the questionnaire indicated sporadic excessive alcohol use. The client received a mandatory referral to the alcoholism counselor. If the counselor at that time would have questioned the man about his alcohol abuse, or attempted to send him to AA, she would have found a thoroughly resistant client. Resistant, curiously, comes from the Latin word "resisto," meaning "to withstand," which was a functional way of being, contrary to its later meaning. Instead, she paced his verbal and nonverbal manifestations carefully, asking questions about the recent experiences that brought him into treatment and visually and tonally mirrored him, joining his model of the world on every appropriate level. Within a short time, the client's expression of anger disappeared and he actually apologized for his original attitude. At that point, knowing that rapport had been established, the counselor began using the second principle of rapport skills—leading.

LEADING

Leading assumes that the therapist has the knowledge of what he wants to accomplish in the treatment session. It is useful to have a rather specific objective although the therapist requires a great amount of flexibility in reaching this objective since the chances of success of the intervention increase accordingly. Meeting a contract, goal or outcome in alcoholism treatment is far from linear and the process of reaching that goal needs to be continually adjusted to the needs of the client in order to maintain rapport. However, early on it is of the essence to determine the final results of the intervention in the terms of the client. Let me present some basic premises for this. Elsewhere in this monograph I postulated and then demonstrated how the human organism naturally moves toward well being given that the right conditions are established for internal choice. Pacing is the first way by which the therapist creates internal choice since understanding and acceptance naturally bring about changes in internal representation of self. However, at that point, the changes do not contain a prescription for moving toward continued sobriety and well being. Leading is what consciously, on the part of the therapist, and unconsciously frequently on the part of the alcoholic occurs in the creation of a well formed outcome and finally a compelling future. Yeager states:

> Leading is somewhat like writing an outline for a term paper or an article in your head that outlines the directions of the conversation in advance. Having a mental map allows the therapist to stay on course as the mutual goal is pursued. Leading the client's attention and interests in specific directions call for specific techniques.[7]

Leading techniques in NLP terminology contain one or more of the following elements:

Translating. Bringing the alcoholic from limited or constricted communication to a way of being expressive, i.e., if the client is not in touch with his feelings or cannot talk about them, can he describe more comfortably how he perceives (visual) the situation? It is often essential for a productive start-up in an intervention with an alcoholic to bridge gaps from one representational system (visual, auditory, or kinesthetic) to another one. Translating from one modality to another as a treatment tool creates understanding and appreciation, which again solidifies the rapport. A rather humorous example involves a note I left our housekeeper, underlining a specific word because I was concerned that she might forget a particular item. When I came home that night, she angrily stated, showing me the note, "You did not have to yell at me!"

Anchoring to locations, gestures, tones, feelings, and images can elicit a desired response at a particular point in the intervention. Dilts describes it as "a technique used to reprogram and resequence internal and external response."[8] Anchors, like all NLP principles, are natural phenomena. Every human being has a set of anchors, triggers that were installed sometime during his lifetime. A particular song, reminding you of your first love is an anchor, a particular smell that brings the Sunday afternoon meals of early childhood to mind is one, and so is a spouse's backrub which reminds you of a parent consoling you after a hard day at school. Anchors are of course prevalent phenomena in alcoholism. Particular triggers may set a drinking sequence in motion regardless of the stated motivation and decision of the alcoholic. When working with a highly motivated female alcoholic in early sobriety, it appeared that while she was at work, she was really motivated to be sober. However, by the time she got home, she would walk to the liquor cabinet, pour herself a drink, kick off her shoes, and put her feet on the cocktail table. Upon closer examination in turned out that, when going home, she was fine until she put her hands on the steering wheel. At that time, the image as described above would flash into her mind and from that point on, the anchor being released, she would follow the image right into reality. Initially, much of the therapy was therefore focused on "detaching" the sequence from the anchor and leading the client to a new internal set of instructions once the original anchor (hands on the steering wheel) was released. Yeager states:

> The same stimulus equals the same response each time unless the context or frame changes . . . anchors produce instant replay . . . (Thus NLP has created anchoring as the process of) . . . installing the habit of choice – a compelling choice that is a well-formed outcome.[9]

Tonal leading. While during the pacing phase of rapport the therapist will in its essential form match a client, during the leading part the therapist will make those voice changes that allow for a more productive state of mind in the client. For example, an alcoholic, sober three weeks sighs deeply and in a soft, low, slow voice states, "I'll never make 90 days." The counselor first matches the voice, but once rapport has been established, raises his voice level, and the rhythm of his tone. The client is able to follow and surprises himself by verbally affirming some of the ways he has recently learned in AA that produce continued sobriety.

Visual leading. An example is an alcoholic who states he is depressed and his body posture clearly indicates that this is so: hunched shoulders, chin pointed at chest, hands listlessly on lap, face without expression. After pacing for some time, the counselor sits up straight, brings his shoulders back and uses some gestures while talking. At that point, the client's breathing goes higher in the chest, some color returns to his face and he slowly begins talking. Frequently, auditory and visual leading can be used most successfully in combination, but its final success depends to an important extent on the preceding pacing, mirroring, or matching.

OUTCOME FRAMING

As stated previously, an essential aspect of successful leading is a process called outcome framing, treated extensively in the NLP literature.[10,11,12] Outcomes may be described as the goals specified as the desired state of mind or performance. The NLP approach is to define outcomes that can be verified in sensory terms and that are specific enough to generate a shared observation and agreement of their achievement. According to Dilts, NLP is "highly outcome oriented . . . and . . . the initial and most important step in any therapeutic interaction is the identification and definition of the outcome."[13] The outcome is presented in conditions of well-formedness and as therapists it is important to impose these conditions on clients so that a natural moving toward well being may take place.

What are the four well-formedness conditions?

1. The outcome must be stated in the positives. The unconscious mind has difficulties operating according to negatives (I invite you not to think of a blue giraffe) which makes it essential for a goal to be stated as attaining/maintaining sobriety, instead of not getting drunk, keeping one's equilibrium, sense of self, etc., or instead of not getting so angry anymore, to state serenity or peacefulness as a goal. It is, in general, much easier to design a way for a client to operate toward a positive outcome than away from a negative one in terms of naturally moving toward well being. Frequently, clients and even therapists have a very difficult time describing what they want instead of what is undesirable.

The problem is in essence that if the unconscious mind only has information about what is not wanted, it has no place to move toward since there is no place in the mind called "neutral." Since this double bind command creates increased internal anxiety, chances are that the behavior the client seeks to eliminate then actually is reinforced. The reason is that it becomes an even stronger anchor in the context of the client's survival skills. Stating outcomes in positive terms eliminates ambiguity on unconscious levels.

2. The outcome or desired state must be within the client's control. Dilts states, "One of the major goals of NLP is to put the focus of control with respect to achieving the outcome with the client,"[14] i.e., instead of the alcoholic stating, "I want my wife to stop nagging," the statement, when reframed within his control becomes, "I would like to handle myself (in a chosen way) when my wife, etc.," or the therapist may ask what the alcoholic might consider doing that would assist that outcome. The importance of this well-formedness condition is not so much the issue of being responsible for self, but to begin to let the alcoholic client know the advantages of being in the driver's seat, the possibility of a sense of self, or personal competence, of finally, in some ways, being in charge of the self again.
3. The outcome must meet the criteria of ecology. For instance, a female client stopped drinking but received few skills to deal with severe anxiety that became strong in sobriety. Since drinking had reduced her anxiety level, the ecology of treatment required the creation of additional internal resources in sobriety to lower the client's anxiety level. Even though the sobriety outcome was appropriate, no provisions had been made for her to deal with tension and anxiety in abstinence. The positive by-products of her drinking had been ignored. The purpose of meeting the criteria of ecology is to orient the therapist and the client toward considering possible future impacts of the outcome and to accommodate for this impact during the intervention. This is also part of a process called future pacing which means connecting the client's outcomes achieved in the therapist's office to his actual reality.

4. The outcome must be testable and demonstrated in sensory experience. Both the alcoholic and the counselor must be able to perceive and evaluate progress toward an outcome. Given that success builds on itself, it is important for the alcoholic to be able to perceive his progress. It also maintains rapport between client and therapist, since both have a similar way of measuring this progress as opposed to an alcoholic stating, "I don't have to come here anymore because I feel happy," which is not measurable in the therapist's experience unless the client and therapist have made some clear agreements about what "happy" looks, sounds, and feels like. In outcome framing there is a requirement for being able, in some way, to clearly define "happy." Once the outcome is testable and demonstrable in the client's personal experience, it can be future paced, in a sense anchored to the client's reality. As an example, an alcoholic would leave the therapist's office feeling motivated to remain sober, but would start drinking within two days after the appointment. After several weeks of this reoccurring, the therapist began to focus on future pacing the client's motivation. One established form of future pacing is role playing. The therapist, in role play, moved the client day by day through staying sober until they came to the day of the next session. The client, perceiving himself sober visually, auditory, and kinesthetically, was able to use the role play as a bridge, the future pace to reality, and maintained sobriety.

SUMMARY AND CONCLUSION

NLP places much emphasis on rapport skills, in effect credits successful intervention with being solidly based on firmly established skills on the level of visual, auditory, and kinesthetic representations and obtains and uses high quality information based on these models by carefully calibrating such measurable observations as posture, gestures, facial expression, tone (rate, rhythm, pitch), and breathing. Once the therapist matches or mirrors the client, he can begin leading the client to an outcome that adheres to the well-formedness conditions. Leading is accomplished by a variety of methods such as anchoring, translating, use of tonal and visual leads, and the elements of outcome framing which includes the process of future pacing. Of course, the ultimate purpose of rapport skills is to move the alcoholic toward his outcome or his desired state, the achievement of continuous sobriety coupled with an internal state of well being that will allow him to achieve his true personal goals.

REFERENCES

1. Yeager, J., *Thinking About Thinking With NLP*, p. 57.
2. Cameron-Bandler, L., *Solutions*, p. 32.
3. Ibid, p. 34.
4. Ibid, p. 34.
5. Yeager, J., unpublished seminar worksheet, 1984.
6. Cameron-Bandler, L., *Solutions*, p. 39.
7. Yeager, J., *Thinking About Thinking With NLP*, p. 26.
8. Dilts, R., *Applications of Neuro-Linguistic Programming*, p. 44.
9. Yeager, J., *Thinking About Thinking With NLP*, p. 27-28.
10. Cameron-Bandler, L., *Solutions*, p. 89.
11. Dilts, R., *Applications of Neuro-Linguistic Programming*, p. 35.
12. Bandler, R. and J. Grinder, *Reframing*, p. 61.
13. Dilts, R., *Applications of Neuro-Linguistic Programming*, p. 33.
14. Ibid, p. 38.
15. Ibid, p. 36.

Chapter 4

Neuro-Linguistic Programming and the Family in Alcoholism Treatment

Donald I. Davis, MD

SUMMARY. What are the central family issues in alcoholism, and how can NLP be used to help deal with them in alcoholism treatment? These are the topics of this paper.

FAMILY ISSUES

Significant relationships (a term which will be used interchangeably with family here) interact cybernetically with alcoholic behavior in the individual in such a way that the abuse of alcohol and the relationships affected by it are inextricably intertwined. Other people have not been proven to cause the alcoholic to become dependent, but once he or she is, others play an active role in the perpetuation of dependence, and are in turn adversely affected by the alcohol use they enable. Furthermore, relationships, which form the third element of the destructive tetrad (alcoholic, significant others, relationships between alcoholics and others and others and others, and the alcohol itself) invariably suffer when one person is drinking excessively. I have described the family issues in alcoholism at great length elsewhere.[1] There is now an extensive descriptive literature of what it is like to grow up in a family with an alcoholic parent.[2,3,4,5] There is also some observational research data documenting that the presence of or absence of alcohol in an alcoholic family consistently is associated with certain relationship differences, such as physical distance between family members.[6] For our purposes here, we shall simply summarize the key family tasks to be accomplished in successful alcoholism treatment, pre- and post-abstinence.

Pre-abstinence. The primary task of family members is to emotionally detach from the alcoholic's alcohol using behavior enough to remain in the relationship—while foregoing overreactions that used to provide excuses for drinking and while pursuing one's own emotional, relationship, vocational, physical, and spiritual development in a healthy way. Sometimes there are beliefs held by certain family members, e.g., the belief of a spouse who is herself an adult child of an alcoholic that this is the way life is, that need to be overcome. If so, belief change may be a prerequisite task for family members, as it often is a critical issue for the alcoholic him or herself.[7]

Post-abstinence. The chief relationship task is to minimize old patterns that used to serve as cues for drinking, while developing whatever new individual and interactional communication skills are needed to allow all family members to grieve for the lost opportunities caused by drinking and to move on to improved problem-solving skills and greater intimacy. There may also be the additional task of finding alternative behaviors, other than drinking, to serve certain key functions alcohol use had come to serve in the family. The option is to help the family gain the resources that will make that function unnecessary.[8]

NEURO-LINGUISTIC PROGRAMMING (NLP) IN FAMILY TREATMENT

In working for sixteen years in a variety of contexts, and with an integrative approach to family therapy, with families of alcoholics, and adding NLP approaches in the past eight of these years, I have found that NLP offers multiple means of facilitating accomplishing the central relationship tasks of alcoholism treatment described above. Ignoring the risk of trivializing NLP, I would propose that there are (at least) four distinct ways in which NLP can be drawn upon to facilitate family therapy for alcoholism. The first regards the presuppositions that provide the substratum in which we cultivate change in therapy. There are certain presuppositions of NLP that establish a particularly positive atmosphere, which is nowhere more important than in working with alcoholic families. The second involves the contributions of NLP to enhancement of rapport skills. In addition to the obvious need for the therapist to be highly skilled at establishing rapport with multiple family members, there is often more than the usual need for (rapid) learning of rapport skills by family members in a family of an alcoholic. A third way NLP helps is through use of methods for changing state rapidly. This is the most obvious, dramatic, and probably easiest to learn aspect of NLP and has frequent application for installing more resourceful response states where previously more rigid, limiting habitual behaviors recurred in interactions between family members. The fourth way to draw upon NLP with alcoholic families is for changing limiting beliefs. Here NLP offers a myriad of approaches ranging from artfully crafted single statement reframes to multi-step reimprinting or outcome framing language patterns.

PRESUPPOSITIONS

NLP rests on certain presuppositions, too extensive to review here.[9] Certain of them provide a particularly useful framework for working with alcoholic families. First and foremost among them for our purposes is "feedback versus failure." That is, whatever happens in response to one's own initiated efforts is useful information, i.e., feedback, even if it is not what was desired and could be construed as a failure, such as taking a drink (a "slip") by a recovering alcoholic. In working with substance abusers, this feedback frame of reference is equally as valuable for the therapist as it is for family members. As it is often said in Alcoholics Anonymous (AA), in alcoholism treatment, the goal is longer and longer periods of sobriety. That means slips are to be expected. But that is very discouraging to therapists and family alike, unless they have been prepared to genuinely treat these slips as sources of information about what still has to be accomplished in an ever-improving process. Since the mere presence of alcohol can reinstitute a whole old set of previously learned family interactional patterns in a newly recovering family, giving up in despair is a common reaction of spouses or children or parents of substance abusers who slip. Their whole world seems as bad as it used to be. The feedback frame of reference helps everyone to hold onto the detachment that is so vital, to be able to pursue personal growth in the face of a loved one's renewed drinking and even to look at a slip with curiosity about its unique precipitants. The concomitant sustaining of hopefulness then also translates into more successful support for the alcoholic to stop the renewed drinking sooner.

There are two other presuppositions of NLP that I find most helpful with families of alcoholics. One is that we all have the resources necessary either to do or to learn to do what we need to do. Since members of families with an alcoholic often come in demoralized and ashamed and feeling inadequate, this frame is often a necessary one for reassurance that they can change. The other presupposition is that the meaning of what we say is in the response that we get. That is, how people take what was said, or how it was said, determines what will follow more than does the intent of the speaker; therefore, the meaning is the response. In the family in which one or more members is frequently in an altered state of consciousness, communication has usually become abysmal. There is a lot of blaming and little personal responsibility taken for the failure to resolve issues. The presupposition, the meaning is the response, applied in sessions, at first by means of frequent interruptions to remind people to take the response they just got as feedback and then take responsibility for finding out how they might restate themselves in such a way that will get themselves understood in the way they want to be understood, provides a face-saving framework for learning to take more personal responsibility for the impact of one's behavior. Once practiced in sessions, assignments can be given to schedule whole discussions at home based on the presupposition that the meaning is the response. "Fair fighting" guidelines such as making I statements and staying in the present rather than dragging up the past can, of course, be embedded within this broader framework. Always important, personal responsibility is essential in the alcoholic system in which denial and dissociation and blaming have been installed over time as necessary mechanisms of pre-abstinence survival.

COMMUNICATION AND RAPPORT SKILLS

Pre-abstinence. The challenge to the therapist working with families with an alcoholic is to be both sufficiently confronting and sufficiently supportive, while maintaining enough rapport with alternately denying and warring factions to keep everybody engaged in the process of change.

Post-abstinence. There is often a great deal of communication skill and ability to recognize and accept difference in others that family members need to learn because they failed to learn them while surviving the drinking. NLP offers a variety of efficient ways to establish rapport or regain rapport after confrontation, as well as ways to improve communication, and these ways are readily teachable to family members.

Basic NLP approaches to modeling, or stepping into, someone else's behavior to understand their experience more fully enable a therapist to convey accurate empathy and "pace" other's well. This is the essence of rapport building. It is a fundamental part of all therapeutic relationships. With couples or larger families, especially with a still actively drinking alcoholic, the therapist's ability to be in or regain rapport is truly put to the test. In the alcoholic family, rapport usually comes about only through either mutual arguing or mutual denial ("let's drop it," etc.) Knowing how to say "let's keep talking about it" (e.g., about the consequences of the present use of alcohol in the relationship(s) and still retain or recover rapport is the challenge, both to the therapist and to each family member who might dare to break with the conventional denial. The NLP attention to predicates of speech and eye accessing cues (to enable pacing each individual's current primary mode of representing their thoughts-auditory, visual, kinesthetic, or olfactory-gustatory), and attention to matching or mirroring body posture and tone and tempo of speech of each separate individual in the family allows the therapist to more safely walk the line between anger and fear among members of an alcoholic family. In my experience, this increases the odds of the family coming back, which numerous outcome studies have shown is itself associated with a higher rate of success in achieving and maintaining abstinence.

Teaching family members to recognize their differences in communication styles and to pace well and bridge these differences often greatly facilitates intimacy and personal growth in the post-abstinence family, which in turn seems to decrease the likelihood of slips.

Establishing rapport ideally also involves effectiveness in sharing communications, so that each party to a discussion senses, correctly, that the other(s) understands him or her accurately. In the alcoholic family accustomed to denial and blaming, mind reading (or guessing one another's thoughts and feelings and righteous pronunciations) are frequent and make a mockery of the concept of effectively shared communications. Modeling as well as teaching the use of the NLP "meta model" patterns, which Grinder and Bandler so elegantly delineated in the 1970s,[10,11] to fill in deletions in one's explanations and challenge modal operators such as "shoulds," has much to contribute to effectiveness of family communication, and is nowhere more consistently needed than in alcoholic families. Such questions as, "What specifically do you mean?" and "How do you know that that is the right way?"—asked within the context of good verbal and body analog rapport—set a useful and needed example.

One other component of NLP, the application of which can be used to greatly facilitate rapport and communication in dysfunctional family systems, is "metaprograms." This still evolving part of NLP, which was first largely promulgated by Leslie Cameron-Bandler and primarily taught in workshops rather than in writing, deals with parameters that measure "differences that make a difference" in what makes each of us unique. One of the early features of this innovative approach to the study of the "self" was the identification of sets of filters, each having to deal with a different dimension of experience by which we sort out information in our world. These were termed the "sorting principles." Do we attend to what is present or what is missing? Do we notice the present first, or are we most attentive to the past, or the future? Do we sort for information, people, aesthetics of place, activity, or cost first in choosing a place to go? These choices and more are made in a characteristic way by each of us and distinguish us from even others in our own families. Utilizing this knowledge (or reframe) among family members in distress, for example in families with an alcoholic member, fosters acceptance of difference and empowers members to better deal with one another as different, rather than be locked into alternating efforts to change one another or capitulate.

HABIT CHANGE

Among the family members of the pre-abstinent alcoholic, the most consistent need is for alternatives to the automatic, enabling behaviors that occur in relationship to the alcoholic's use of alcohol. In Alcoholics Anonymous (Al Anon), this is referred to as the need for detachment. Through the concept of anchoring and the ensuing specific methods for installing more resourceful internal states and behaviors where previously more rigid and limiting responses regularly occur, NLP has provided certain rapid approaches to facilitate healthy detachment in family members of alcoholics. While I have not kept an exact count, I personally have had probably over fifty care examples of successful anchoring of an appropriate, detached state in family members of actively drinking alcoholics. Some have been adults, some children. Some have been in Al Anon or Alateen, some have refused self-help groups. In all cases, the response has been beneficial for the family member and usually has fostered a useful adaptation by others in the family, including the alcoholic. Most commonly, but not exclusively, I have used an anchoring technique (or the shift in submodalities of mental representation known as the swish pattern, which can as rapidly install an alternative, conditioned response) with wives of alcoholic men, wives who already have the ability to act appropriately assertive in the interest of their own and other's well being in some context, e.g., setting limits with their children or in their paid jobs, but who do not apply these resources with their alcoholic husbands. By appropriately assertive, I mean able to represent themselves well verbally, without hostility, but with firmness, and stay in a discussion where there is some difference of opinion until one knows she has been heard out, she has listened effectively to the other person, and she has not given in prematurely. When a woman who, inadvertently, has been enabling her spouse's alcohol abuse by overreacting with anger, changing her plans, nagging, covering up the hurt from his drinking behavior, sobbing, withdrawing to her room, etc., learns from Al Anon or whatever means that works how to remain sufficiently detached from her partner's drinking to go about attending well to her own and her family's needs, and to do so without providing any excuses for his further drinking, things change. The alcoholic is faced with himself and the consequences of his own behavior in a way that one might say fosters more rapidly hitting his own personal bottom, that point of self-destruction below which he is not willing to go. Imagine the impact on the family when that happens after not six or more months of Al Anon but only one hour of therapy! Yet this is how anchoring techniques and swish patterns work, rapidly. Fortunately, a fundamental tenet of NLP is to always check out the ecological consequences of changing from the present state to some desired state, preferably before making a change. Another way of stating this in NLP jargon is that one of the conditions of a well-formed statement of a desired outcome is that the desired state must preserve the positive byproduct of the present state. For example, in the alcoholic family system it is important to check in advance at least with the spouse with whom one is working as to whether the present enabling, or alcohol abuse maintaining, behaviors are necessary to protect this spouse from even greater, e.g., physical, abuse. It would be essential then that any new response state contain within it the capacity to act in ways that also avoid physical abuse. I generally spend considerably more time exploring with spouses, or children, of heavy drinkers both what appropriate assertiveness and detachment might be for them and what might happen if they could routinely act with those resources then I need to spend helping them install the new resource state once they've decided they know the worst that might follow from this change, and they want to make it anyway.

Working with more than one person in the family at a time when using such rapid and powerful individual NLP change techniques is both more humane and potentially more productive than working just with the individual. Human nature is such that typically when one person in a system steps out of a dance pattern others get confused, and initially do more of their old behaviors or do them more intensely or both for a time until they finally realize the other person is truly never going to fall back into the old steps. Only then do they begin to adapt. When the others actually observe and comprehend the change process, and ideally are part of testing it out promptly, they can begin their adaptations right away, with help, productively.

Post-abstinence. There are usually still some habits that need changing within the family. An interesting pattern, that may be easy to change with good rapport and simple anchoring or submodality swish pattern techniques, is the conditioned response by children or spouse to a particular look or tone of voice of the alcoholic—a look or sound that used to be associated with out of control drinking behavior but may now be part of a benign state. While the change may be easy to make, whether it is made or not is no trivial matter. The persistence of old fear responses in family members can be the additional straw that breaks the back of the now abstinent alcoholic's resolve to stay sober. Stopping drinking is of much less significance than maintaining sobriety and resuming personal growth. The newly abstinent alcoholic is often disappointed by the lack of expected appreciation, acceptance, and warmth coming from his or her family. Only last year, I had three new couples in a two month period come to see me who all told the same story, of husband's extended (6 to 24 months) post 28-day alcohol treatment program sobriety that failed to last because "nothing improved" in the relationship, "so why bother not drinking?" The wives, and the children in one of the cases, had continued to respond to their now sober husbands with distrust, but not the healthy distrust that says, "work with me to see how much better we can be." Rather, theirs was a distrust born of fear of engaging with their newly sober husbands in the process of change. The result was intense boredom all around, and increasing unspoken but nonetheless communicated thoughts that "maybe some things were better when I (he) was drinking." Once again in periods of sobriety, this time these couples are addressing their relationships, in therapy, together. And a major factor that seems to have kept them in therapy was the facilitation, through anchoring in appropriate resources from work or child-rearing, of access to effective response states in the wives to cope with normal levels of disagreement from their husbands. What they had originally rationalized as lack of interest in or hope from pursuing something with their husbands, after installing new responses these women now saw as having been automatic self-intimidation. Having installed and mentally rehearsed these new resources with husbands present as observers further accelerated the successful change process because these husbands became both more believers in the possibility of change and more understanding of the adaptations their wives had made to them while drinking and the consequent subtle destructiveness there had been to their relationships. Children, of course, make similar adaptations to a parent's drinking behavior. Elsewhere, I have previously described using anchoring, within the context of family therapy sessions, to install and test out the effectiveness of more useful resource states in children who used to cringe when a drinking father scolded them and, later, still cringed when a now sober father quite appropriately set limits with them.[12] In short, just as anchoring can be used to expedite achieving a vigilant detachment and appropriate assertiveness in the pre-abstinent family, so can it be used to speed the acquisition of calmness within the context of appropriate mutual problem-solving in post-abstinent families.

NLP approaches to rapidly substituting states and behaviors where previously more limiting ones automatically occurred also has great application to adult children of alcoholics (ACOAs). NLP with ACOAs will be dealt with at length in other papers, but some mention should be made here that some spouses of active alcoholics, and some alcoholics, are themselves ACOAs. When this is the case, the issues are similar to those already discussed, only often more intense. The need for, and benefits of, rapid access to resourceful states such as calmness, detachment, and assertiveness are great. In addition, there may be a prior need to overcome the reactions to or denial, of recollections of abuse of selves or others as children. Sometimes only eliminating a phobic type of response to a childhood memory will permit the rest of the family's recovery to proceed. I have found the NLP fast phobia approach (essentially involving the subject viewing the traumatic memory from a sufficiently dissociated mind frame to tolerate seeing it from before it began until just after it is all over, followed by associating into the frame after it is all over and moving it backwards rapidly) of great help in easing these ACOAs into tolerating discussing the issues they used to avoid but now must deal with in their new families in recovery. As necessary, major changes in ability to forgive others, self-acceptance, and their belief systems in general then can be pursued, using variations of anchoring patterns and visualization to remake their own memories of personal history and change the paradigmatic experiences that imprinted in them the now limiting beliefs about themselves and nature of the world around them. With these thoughts, we begin to move into the realm of the last major category of our discussion, that of belief change.

BELIEF CHANGE (AND IDENTITY)

Self-acceptance, empowerment, generosity and flexibility in accepting differences in significant others, a spiritual oneness with the universe, these are the highest pursuits for profound recovery from alcoholism or from a family member's alcoholism. Of course, these are goals that are universally positively correlated with improved health. The alcoholic family's needs are no different from any other's, only harder than some to meet. There are those in the alcoholism treatment field who believe that personal growth for the alcoholic really only resumes after a year or so of abstinence. Their corollary bias is that growth oriented individual, marital, or family psychotherapy should be put off about that long. In my opinion, this is based on a statistically correct, naturalistic analysis of the course of alcoholism recovery in the absence of very effective therapeutic interventions, and not to what need necessarily be the case. It is akin to accepting that psychotherapy, individual or family, is not a good idea pre-abstinence because it used to exclusively be used without attention to the drinking as a primary problem and, therefore, used to contribute to delays in recovery. Whereas, family therapy and individual therapy especially utilizing NLP and Ericksonian approaches, can contribute substantially to speeding recovery when a primary focus is on the achievement of abstinence. Growth oriented individual and relationship work can usefully begin as soon as there are congruent attempts at abstinence. In fact, delaying such work at the relationship level can be very damaging, especially if frequent attendance at AA and/or Al-Anon keep people apart in their limited non-working hours. Relationships in early abstinence can be filled with disappointments. Without support, communications (re)training, and acceptance of differences these relationships can stagnate or deteriorate unnecessarily. With appropriate relationship therapy, trust and intimacy can be (re)established.

Limiting beliefs, e.g., about one's own rights to health or happiness, and an inability to forgive are often rooted in certain paradigmatic early childhood experiences. The types of adaptations that family members make to the alcoholic's drinking behavior incorporate these limitations. The resultant unique distribution of roles in a given family system—super responsible or distracter, etc.,—are in turn maintained by the drinking. There will be a tension in the system post-abstinence that will only be relieved by renewed drinking, a change in how the roles are filled, or the elimination of the need for the roles. The latter is the most profound and generally the most health sustaining change.

Removing these limitations in alcoholic family members, particularly when they were present in spouses who are themselves ACOAs, has seemed to me essential at times to progress in therapy. I have generally used one or another form of NLP reimprint approach. For example there was the ACOA mother who allowed herself to be figuratively walked over by others in her family while she persisted in explaining her way of thinking and plaintively seeking agreement with it. She had grown up in an alcoholic family in which neither parent took the time to seek her opinion or explain anything to her. While simple anchoring of an effective, assertive resource state from her work context had already facilitated her holding to a position without tears, she persisted in her extreme of explaining her position and hearing out others at great cost in time, energy, and respect. She stated repeatedly that she felt compelled to do better than her parents had done with her. By that she meant particularly that she would never discount another in her family as she was discounted. Her belief was that her opinion in the family didn't matter. She was going to see to it that the opinion of others in her family of procreation did matter, no matter how obnoxious they acted. She had several memories of situations from childhood that captured the origins of her underlying belief that her own opinion and wishes were not of value. The earliest one stood out the most. In it she was about age 6 or 7 being told by her parents that she was going for surgery immediately. She recalled no explanation, preparation, or discussion with her about her feelings. Even though she now accepted that the surgery had been necessary, she had never forgiven her mother and alcoholic father for acting that way. Using the type of reimprint approach that Robert Dilts demonstrates in his Belief Systems and Health Workshops, I had her go back in her mind to that childhood memory and change it and then relive it in several new ways. First, in a comfortable state, she observed the memory as if it were on a screen and she dissociated from it, seeing herself in it. She was requested to figure out what each person in the scene—mother, father, her younger self—would have needed to handle that situation optimally. For resources, she was to draw upon all of her current adult life experiences as well as her awareness of the resources and capabilities of others she knew of, as necessary. Having determined what each character needed, and having revised her scene as if they now had these resources to see if they were sufficient, she could then move into the scene and experience from within the scene, associated into it, what it would have been like from each person's position with these new resources. The full sequence of steps was done for one character before moving on to the full sequence for another. For example, she was instructed to find and try out the resources that would have enabled her mother to carry out mother's (presumed) positive intentions (of protecting her health without allowing her drinking and her self-absorption as well as father's to cause a delay). Stepping into that revised mother's role, with adequate nurturing and assertive resources, enabled her to establish for herself a new model for effectiveness as a wife and mother in her present family. Later, repeating the sequence and stepping into her younger self miraculously already having adult resources for coping with and understanding the situation, she concluded with tears of relief that she felt much more self-acceptance in that childhood behavior. Evidence of that self-acceptance then readily appeared in her subsequent behavior with her present family, and it has lasted for many months. She still explains and invites input, but she now is succinct, calmer, and more effective.

I have had a number of such cases in which I have used some form of reimprint. The specific technique may vary, such as using submodality shifts in mental imagery to more rapidly provide resource states to utilize in changing the experiences of the memory, but the belief change objective and acceptance of self and/or ability to forgive others and move on is the same. This type of approach has seemed essential to me in at least two cases in which the abused spouse of an alcoholic was herself an ACOA who was as a child sexually molested by her father. The approach for such people has built into it relatively safe ways to reexperience the often hitherto forgotten abuse incidents and to achieve a sufficiently empowered state to begin to act in one's own interest without undue hostility, within a present abusive relationship.

Other aspects of NLP that have much to contribute to growth oriented work with families of alcoholics are so extensive that it would require a textbook to enumerate them fully. And their applications are so ubiquitous as to make a few examples too simplistic. For brevity, I will say only that alcoholic families pre-abstinence have more than the average need to change their beliefs about what is possible, and who they are, and how they fit into what kind of world, and that post-abstinence, they have at least the average need for healthy evolution that everyone else has. The fundamental linguistic patterns of NLP, first put forth in *Structure of Magic, Volumes I and II* as the Metamodel, and later elaborated into well formedness conditions for stipulating one's outcome as well as into advanced language patterns, are continually useful to the therapist confronted with these families. Having the skills to clarify deleted, denied, projected, and distorted statements rapidly, to specify goals well and teach how to specify they well, to reframe incisively, and to break up a belief by responding at a metalevel with a response that contains an incompatible presupposition makes the process of therapy a little more helpful for those of us too impatient to otherwise tolerate continuing to work with these admittedly difficult families. And if we don't work with them, many of them don't do very well. Hopefully the time will come soon when we can document better that NLP has enhanced family therapy for alcoholism and that that makes a difference in alcoholism treatment outcome.

REFERENCES

1. Davis, D.I. *Alcoholism treatment: An integrative family and individual approach*. NYC: Gardner Press, 1987.

2. Wegscheider, S. *Another chance: Hope and health for the alcoholic family*. Palo Alto, CA: Science and Behavior Books, 1980.

3. Black, C. *It will never happen to me: Children of alcoholics as youngsters, adolescents and adults*. Denver: Medical Administration Co., 1982.

4. Woititz, J. *Adult Children of Alcoholics*. Pompano, Beach, FL: Health Communications, Inc., 1983.

5. Gravitz, H.L. and Bowden, J. *Guide to recovery: A book for adult children of alcoholics*. Holmes Beach, FL: Learning Publications, Inc., 1985.

6. Steinglass, P., Bennett, L.A., Wolin, S.J., and Reiss, D., *The Alcoholic Family*. NYC: Basic Book, Inc., 1987.

7. Davis, D.I. *Op. Cit.*, Chapter 12.

8. Davis, D.I., Berenson, D., Steinglass, P. and Davis, S.L.R., "The adaptive consequences of drinking." *Psychiatry, 37*: 209-215, 1974. Reprinted in *Annual Alcoholism Review*, N.J.: Rutgers Univ., 1979. Revised version reprinted in Davis, D.I., *Op. cit.*

9. Davis, D.I. and Davis, S.L.R., "Integrating individual and family therapy using Neuro-Linguistic Programming." *Int. J. Family Psychiatry 6(1)*: 5-9, 1985.

10. Bandler, R. and Grinder, J. *The Structure of Magic I: A book about language and therapy*. Palo Alto, CA: Science and Behavior Books, Inc., 1975.

11. Grinder, J. and Bandler, R. *The structure of magic II: A book about communication and change*. Palo Alto, CA: Science and Behavior Books, Inc., 1975.

12. Davis, D.I. "I need help to stop drinking: An integrative family therapy approach to the management of a family in early recovery." Chapter in Kaufman, E. (ed.). *Family Case studies in the treatment of alcoholism*. NYC: Gardner Press, 1984. Revised version reprinted in Davis, D.I., *Op. cit.*, Chapter 13.

Chapter 5

An Application of Hypnotic Communication to the Treatment of Addictions

Jeffrey M. Doorn, MA, CAC

SUMMARY. The application of hypnotic communication to the treatment of addiction can allow for a successful integration of the "resistant" client into the treatment experience. Serving the self in some capacity, the addiction, is viewed as a resource to the client. This perspective gives rise to a treatment approach that emphasizes the development of a cooperative relationship with the client, to create a context within which change can occur. Clinical examples are provided to highlight the application of hypnotic principles and techniques.

The treatment of addictions has long been plagued with a rigidity that is characteristic of the disease it seeks to remedy. This rigidity is evident when clients are expected to placidly conform to treatment without remnants of the denial, distortion, and minimization that are symptomatic of their illness. Unfortunately, these symptoms are also coupled with an extremely constricted awareness of options, which often interferes with an individuals ability to utilize treatment. The manner in which a counselor addresses these manifestations of addiction will largely determine the climate of the therapeutic relationship.

Client's negative or contrary reactions to treatment are frequently perceived by counselors as indicators of a client's lack of willingness or readiness for treatment. The inability to use "resistant" responses may foster an adversarial relationship between counselor and client. This cat and mouse relationship is a clear sign that the counselor is now a part of rather than apart from the addicted system. Predictably, the more responsibility the counselor assumes for the client's recovery, the more the client reacts in a helpless, out of control, or underfunctioning manner (Bepko & Krestan, 1980). This pattern of interaction can easily frustrate counselors. Consequently, counselors often experience feelings of inadequacy, while their clients are trapped behind an ever thickening wall of defensiveness.

Milton H. Erickson, MD, was noted for practicing a unique form of therapy that integrated hypnotic communication with psychotherapy. His writings indicate a skillful use of verbal and non-verbal communication which can be effectively applied to counseling addicted individuals (Erickson, 1980). Employing the principles and techniques of hypnotic communication can increase a counselor's flexibility in dealing with the challenges of addiction treatment. Powerful methods of establishing rapport, initiating change, and facilitating a future orientation, can be borrowed from Erickson's work to enhance a counselor's ability to promote change within the addicted system. The study of the following hypnotic principles and techniques allows for a richer and more varied approach to the treatment of addictions.

ELICITING COOPERATION

To gain a client's cooperation Erickson utilized a client's own communication patterns to elicit rapport between himself and the client (Gilligan, 1987). When people are in rapport with each other such matching of output happens naturally and spontaneously at an unconscious level. Output can also be matched consciously by counselors who are willing to attend to a client's experience. Erickson referred to this procedure as "pacing" (Bandler and Grinder, 1975). In order to pace a client's experience, a counselor must match his or her own verbal and non-verbal communications to the client's output.

There are many aspects of a person's experience that can be paced. Erickson often matched the non-verbal portions of the client's experience because this tended to bypass conscious resistance. Such aspects as respiration rate, eye blink rate, the tone and tempo of voice, and significant gestures were often paced.

There are also verbal methods of matching a client's experience.

"Pacing" statements can be used to elicit rapport and simultaneously initiate a pattern of agreement between counselor and client. Trance inductions are often started simply by describing a client's on-going experience.

> While you sit there you can feel the chair beneath you, as you continue to breathe . . . in . . . and . . . out . . . hearing my voice as you continue to listen . . .

Each of the above phrases is intended to validate an element of the client's experience. The description of the client's breathing is timed to coincide with the client's actual breathing. The hypnotist's description must match the client's experience in order to pace the client successfully.

Pacing statements are not only based on observable behavior but also on what the counselor can logically infer about the client's experience.

> . . . and as you continue to listen you can notice certain aspects of your experience your attention can drift or stay focused as you continue to breathe . . .

Verbal pacing initiates a pattern of agreement, known to hypnotists as a "yes set" (Erickson, Rossi & Rossi, 1976). This creates a positive psychological momentum increasing the probability that a suggestion will be followed.

> . . . recognizing those sensations that you feel every day, noticing that you really do breathe in quite a regular fashion as you listen to the sound of my voice, hearing these words you can begin to feel more secure . . .

Except for the last phrase all of the above statements are intended as "pacing" statements. Each phrase provides a description of experience with which the client can identify and agree. Several "pacing" statements are used to elicit a pattern of agreement before a suggestion is offered. In this instance an experience of greater security was suggested.

The following is a brief example from an intake session demonstrating how pacing can be used to establish rapport and gain a client's cooperation.

> Charlie, as you sit there in that chair, and hear my voice, knowing that this is a new situation for you. You have never been here before, and you have never met me. I know very little about you. I wonder as we continue to talk if you can keep track to make sure that I ask you all the questions that you think are relevant to you being here.

Counselors must join with a client's psychological reality in order to expand the self-limiting boundaries that bind the client to addiction. Clients are more easily influenced by counselors who demonstrate that they understand the client's view of the world. Pacing demonstrates the counselor's willingness to operate within the client's frame of reference without being judgmental or critical. For the client, rapport is indeed, the experience of being understood and accepted.

Another way the counselor can foster a cooperative relationship with a client is to use words and images that are consistent with the client's own frame of reference (Erickson & Rossi, 1981). A counselor working with a carpenter might use words that would nail down exactly what he or she wanted to say, and thereby, build on the client's ability to make connections within plain but solid language. Counselors can strengthen rapport by using language and associations that are familiar to the client. This allows the counselor to communicate within the client's frame of reference.

UTILIZING RESISTANCE

Utilizing resistance begins with pacing the client's experience. When the client's behavior is accepted as a valid and meaningful expression of some aspect of the client's self, resistance often begins to diminish. Resistance can be thought of as a form of self-protection. It is the client's attempt to protect himself from some perceived threat, either real or imagined. Regardless of how self-destructive a client's behavior appears, it is the best choice given the client's level of awareness at that moment. This does not mean that the counselor encourages or condones the self-destructive behavior, but that the counselor understands the context from which it emerged.

One of the best ways to integrate the resistant client into treatment may be through positive reframing (Watzlawick, Weakland and Fisch, 1974). Rather than attempting to convince the client of his need to change his ways, the counselor orients the client to "considering the disadvantage of change and the exceptional assets of current skills (symptoms) before even contemplating the possibility of change" (Beahrs, 1982, p.116).

> John, I don't think you should really seriously consider stopping drinking until you have a good reason to do this. You're going to be here for about a month. This will give you time to explore whether or not it would benefit you in some way. It will give you time to examine just how useful the drinking has been. How it has helped you to deal with feelings, situations, and other people. I think it is important you consider exactly what it is you would be giving up and what it is you would be getting.

Another technique for dealing with resistant clients is to validate the resistant behavior and then go on to presuppose the coexistence of another more cooperative part of the personality.

> *Client*: I don't want to be here. I don't want to stop drinking.
> *Counselor*: Frank you don't have to want to be here. Unfortunately, the court ordered you here. I'm sure that really has got you steamed.
> *Client*: Nobody can make me stop drinking no matter how long I stay here.
> *Counselor*: You are right Frank nobody can stop you from drinking, the choice will always be yours. Hopefully, when you leave here, you will have a choice to stay sober or not to stay sober. You will make a decision about that. Because just as there is part of you that is very angry about being here, there is another part of you that is viewing this experience objectively and is wondering how much of this really applies to you.

If the client remains resistant the counselor needs to back up and do more pacing and validation of the client's resistance before attempting to lead him or her into new territory.

BUILDING CHOICE

In dealing with addictions it is imperative that the counselor always maintain the stance of building choices rather than restricting them. Unfortunately, clients are often given the impression that the primary goal of treatment is to make them give up something rather than gain something.

The following passage illustrates how an constrictive approach to influencing people may not always be the most productive in achieving results.

> Once I was sitting in a waiting room of a doctor's office and I noticed a father and his small daughter caught in a struggle. It seems that the daughter picked up another visitor's keys and was intent on keeping them. The fathers face was flushed in frustration and the daughter was in tears. The little girl's mother quickly removed a small teddy-bear from her bag and offered it to her. The girl's eyes quickly cleared as she dropped the keys to clutch the furry softness of the stuffed bear.

The little girl's mother somehow knew to offer her an alternative. This changed the tenor of the scenario from control to cooperation, from no choice to greater choice. This is the major difference between a flexible approach to treatment and a more traditional one. "The former works toward solutions by identifying boundaries and expanding them, while the latter attempts to correct 'problems' by restricting the range of self-expressions (e.g., getting the person to stop expressing the symptom)" (Gilligan, p. 20, 1987). A flexible approach to treatment will assist the client in expanding his or her range of choices to include sobriety.

Counselors can greatly enhance their client's ability to take on new challenges by orienting them to their capabilities. Whatever capacities a client possesses can be used as a potential base from which to build an expectation of success. The following out-patient session was with a woman who was in treatment for a period of two years. During this time span she dealt with a variety of issues that had origins stemming from the addicted family system within which she grew up. While she was in out-patient treatment she obtained assistance for two of her adolescent children who were suffering from drug dependence. She participated fully in their in-patient treatment and aftercare. During a previous session she had begun to deal with her own eating disorder.

> *Client*: I never realized I have such a problem with food. I feel so much shame. I've been crying since I started to go to the meetings (Overeaters Anonymous). I can't seem to stay focused.
>
> *Counselor*: Susan, I wonder since things seem hazy, if you could look back to get some clarity. Because Susan, you have already learned a great deal about yourself and about addictions. You know things about denial and about how to work a twelve step program. You're familiar with how sponsors are used and what you are and are not responsible for. You do know about powerlessness and about taking things one day at a time. Susan I wonder with all of the learnings over the past two years, with all of those experiences with treatment, with your experiences in Alcoholics-Anonymous (Al-Anon), Narcotics Anonymous (Nar-Anon), and Adult Children of Alcoholics (ACoA). . . . And the courage it took you to begin setting limits with John and Linda. I wonder if you could take some time and search your mind for what it is that is most important for you to remember right now. What learning would it be most useful for you to be aware of.
>
> *Client* (pauses for a few seconds): Definitely, to take things "one day at a time." I am getting too far ahead of myself. I need to make it simpler and just take my time and go to meetings.

In the above dialogue the counselor attempts to orient the client to her strengths. Her treatment experiences, her involvement in twelve step programs, and her ability to effectively set limits with her children are all powerful learnings that are applicable to her current struggle with her own addiction. Helping clients to access resources of this type facilitates therapeutic change by developing an expectancy of success.

VIEWING ADDICTION AS A RESOURCE

Much treatment time is often spent in helping a client to recognize that his or her life has become unmanageable as a result of the addiction. Unfortunately, what is not stressed often enough is how the addiction made the person's life more manageable in the first place.

Addiction must be understood for its functional aspects. Counselors must have an understanding for how the addiction keeps the client system stable. Treatment needs to address the developmental deficits of the addicted system that may contribute to the continuance of the addiction. For this reason counselors must explore with clients how the addiction functions within the client system. Treatment planning, therefore, must identify the resources needed, and provide experiences that allow the client system to develop alternative choices in these deficit areas.

An illustration of this is a client (Mary) whose co-dependency was manifest in her over-responsible behavior patterns. She had difficulty with the concept of going to meetings in order to learn how to define herself instead of basing her entire existence on her addicted husband. As she started to get better, it became apparent that her over-responsible behavior was a resource in that it protected her from being aware of her feelings of dread, anxiety, and worthlessness. As Mary's involvement in Al-Anon and group therapy continued, she slowly developed a more positive self-concept. Predictably, with improvement in her self-esteem came an abatement in her over-responsible behavior. As her ability to experience and express her feelings improved, she no longer needed to depend upon controlling behavior to avoid or distance from her feelings.

ASSIGNING TASKS

Another method of accessing resources is through assigning small and achievable tasks that are relevant to recovery. What is most important is that the tasks are designed to break the rigid patterns of thinking and behaving which impede a client's recovery. Such tasks should permit the client access to a greater range of options. They should also help expand the restricted model of the world that that person has maintained. Thus the client can begin to develop self-valuing choices rather than the self-devaluing choices of addiction. These tasks often vary in complexity. They could be as simple as asking a client to say "Hello" to three people at a self-help meeting. Contrastingly they could be carefully planned paradoxical symptom prescribing interventions that request that the client perform the symptom as part of an assignment. A client who complained of obsessive thoughts about his or her addiction was given the following prescription.

> For the next three days I want you to be very careful to keep track of time. What I want you to do is this, I want you to obsess about your drug of choice three minutes out of every ten minutes for the next two days. You may need to learn something from reviewing these experiences.

Once the client is able to amplify, attenuate, or alter the symptom in any manner, the character of the problem has changed. The client now has control over the symptom. At this point it is more of a skill than it is a problem. Tasks can be used to initiate a small variation and then build on that change to create positive therapeutic movement (Haley, 1973).

CREATING ILLUSIONS OF CHOICE

Once a positive relationship exists between counselor and client, the counselor may choose to employ therapeutic binds to facilitate constructive movement by that client. Therapeutic binds have been used effectively for ages by parents. Their children being the unwitting recipients of these binding interventions.

> Do you want to say goodnight to your Aunt Jane and Uncle Bill now or after you take your bath.

This statement presupposes that the child is: going to take a bath, and go to bed. At the same time power has been given back to the child for deciding the sequence of events. Simple binds that have been used by addiction counselors include:

> Which Al-Anon meeting would you like to start with. There is one close to here at 7:00 and there is one across town at 8:00.
>
> Since it's Tuesday you'll probably only be able to make four meetings before you start a full week. Now that you have found someone, are you going to ask him to be your sponsor on Tuesday or Thursday.
>
> With your working full-time I think it would be unreasonable to expect yourself to go to more than one N.A. meeting per day during the week. On the weekend you can go to as many as you like.

Each statement contains a presupposition that the person is going to perform the desired task. There is however, room left for freedom of choice in each instance. The client alone decides when or to what extent compliance will be made. When a cooperative relationship has been established, such therapeutic binds tend to facilitate the acceptance of suggestions. Success with this technique is more dependent upon the counselor's commitment to empowering the client, than it is on clever wording. When this technique is employed correctly, the client always senses that permission to refuse any suggestion is within his or her province. This sense of permission enhances the likelihood that suggestions will be taken and keeps responsibility for change in the rightful place—with the client.

> . . . Responsibility for change has always been and will always be with the client. Erickson was very direct about how he saw the role of the client. He maintained that the patient has the ability to do something that will be beneficial and that it is the patient's responsibility to do it. Change cannot be forced upon patients and patients cannot be expected to change in ways that are inappropriate for their needs or foreign to their experiential backgrounds. Unfortunately, this also implies that some patients cannot or will not experience change under any conditions the counselor can create. Counselors who keep the burden of responsibility for change on the shoulders of their patients will have less difficulty recognizing and accepting their impotence in such circumstances. (Havens, 1981)

Utilizing a flexible approach to treatment means that the counselor becomes a student of each particular client's functioning. The counselor therefore, must develop a cooperative relationship with each client in order to explore with the client the view of the world that has been molded by that individual's life experiences. Establishing a positive and cooperative approach to treatment means employing the flexibility and creativity that each counselor possesses in order to tailor treatment to the unique needs of each client. To do this most effectively, the counselor has to focus on the client's abilities and capacity for change. Effective treatment is a process of assisting the client in assuming responsibility for his or her recovery. Further, successful treatment is guided by a future orientation to human functioning, emphasizing where the client is headed rather than where he or she has been.

REFERENCES

Bandler, R. and Grinder, J. *Patterns of the Hypnotic Techniques of Milton H. Erickson, M.D.*, Cupertino, CA: Meta Publications, 1975.

Beahrs, J. *Unity and Multiplicity*, New York, NY: Brunner/Mazel, 1982.

Bepko, C. with Krestan, J. *The Responsibility Trap*, New York, NY: The Free Press, 1985.

Erickson, M. H. and Rossi, E. L. *Experiencing Hypnosis: Therapeutic Approaches to Altered States*, New York, NY: Irvington, 1981.

Erickson, M. H., Rossi, E. L., and Rossi, S. I. *Hypnotic Realities*, New York: Irvington, 1976.

Gilligan, S. *Therapeutic Trances: The Cooperation Principle in Ericksonian Hypnotherapy*, New York, NY: Brunner/Mazel, 1987.

Haley, J. *Uncommon Therapy: The Psychiatric Techniques of Milton H. Erickson, M.D.*, New York, NY: W.W. Norton, 1973.

Havens, R. *The Wisdom of Milton H. Erickson*, New York, NY: Irvington, 1985.

Rossi, E. L. (Ed.). *The Collected Papers of Milton H. Erickson on Hypnosis* (4 vols.), New York, NY: Irvington, 1980.

Watzlawick, P., Weakland, J., and Fisch, R. *Change: Principles of Problem Formation and Problem Resolution*, New York, Norton, 1974.

Chapter 6

A Specific Neuro-Linguistic Programming Technique Effective in the Treatment of Alcoholism

Chelly M. Sterman, MSW, ABECSW, CAC

INTRODUCTION

One of the important Neuro-Linguistic Programming (NLP) presuppositions is that most human beings, unless there is some clearly identifiable malfunction, are born with all the internal resources they may need during their lifetime. That may or may not be true, but if the therapist organizes his work with the client around this principle, the possibilities of moving the alcoholic toward well being appear to be increased. Earlier in this monograph a section was dedicated to human beings' natural tendency to move toward well being giving a sufficient internal repertoire of choices. Thus, it is equally so that at some point, frequently during the formative years, individuals have made major decisions regarding the use of these resources. Often the decisions resulted in actually blocking the use of these resources because of some perceived danger or threat to the individual at an age when information received by the child, because of the source of the life information, was incomplete, inadequate or simply not true. For instance, a child could have been taught, "You cannot trust anybody," which may have been true in his family of origin. However, this is actually not a useful principle in adult life, especially in the establishment of intimate relationships with marriage partners and with one's children. Referring to the previously described principle of "positive intent of behavior versus the actually manifested behavior in the present," the decision to block resources was of course an unconscious action by the child to prevent getting hurt. For example, under the most normal of circumstances, when a child is born, it will cry at some point and not be consoled in some way immediately. Nothing terribly traumatic obviously, but at that point the child may block off a little piece of self, a partial internal resource, that later may function as a guiding life principle. (The first illustration [Figure 1] demonstrates this principle.) From my own experience, at age four I got, in the eyes of a four-year-old, the most exquisite pink dress any four-year-old could ever wish for, so exquisite in fact that I only got to wear it once before it was discovered, a year later, that I had outgrown it. My mother, fully aware of my distress, wished to console me and had a seamstress make a new dress, just like the first one and I waited for it with great anticipation. A short time later I received a beautiful blue dress and was heartbroken. Years later I discovered in my own therapy that what I had extrapolated from this experience was, "I never really get what I want, so make sure you never want something badly." An innocuous enough experience, but the unconscious mind, with its primary function of protecting the human organism, will choose what it considers significant life experiences as its guides. As it turned out, the dress experience became a far more significant element in my life decisions than my parents' divorce some years previously or other seemingly more important events. Graphically, then, in the context of alcoholism treatment, this principle may be demonstrated as follows:

First blocked off internal part as a result of a decision made,	Human organism at birth, the full range of internal resources based on incomplete information early in life.

Blocking resources by closing down parts of oneself continues to occur in the life of the client and his family, many related to relatively normal life events, such as the birth of a new sibling, the move to a new city, the loss of a playmate, the unjust punishment by a teacher, etc., all everyday life situations which guide the child to make decisions that will affect him during his adult life. Thus, by the time he is a teenager, the individual has locked away a number of internal parts containing valuable resources and he is beginning to coast on what now remains: his survival skills. (The second illustration [Figure 2] in this chapter is intended to convey this principle.) Depending on the childhood and the individual's internal resources, the survival skills will be plentiful or constricted, and in the case of an alcoholic, the survival skills will always contain alcohol abuse. Again I refer to this monograph's chapter on NLP as a Conceptual Base in the Treatment of Alcoholism in which a distinction is presented between the positive original intent of the behavior and the present dysfunctional actual behavior. Alcohol use which turns into abuse always had its positive intent rooted in the individual's survival skills. Thus, the intent of the behavior – what it ought to accomplish – determines the continuation of the behavior within

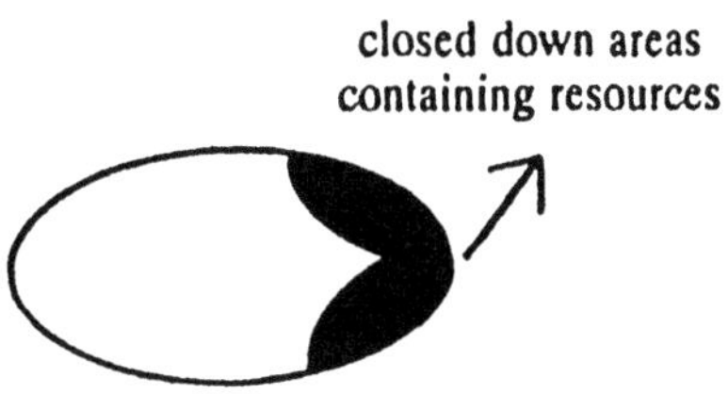

FIGURE 1

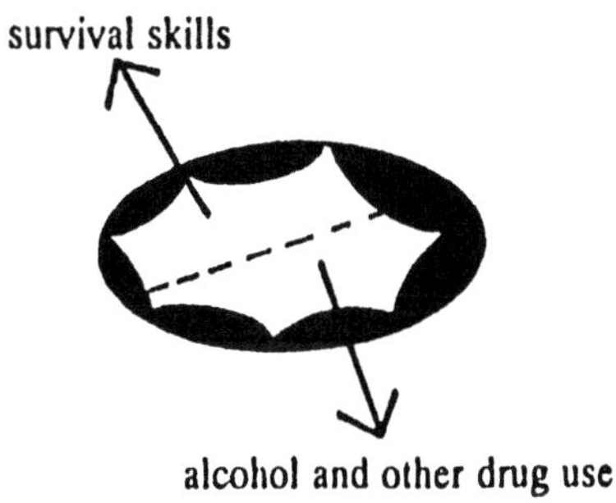

FIGURE 2

the alcoholic's model of the world and not the actual outcome, the internal or external results of the behavior in the present. For instance, when a client closes down in communication with her partner, the intent may be to protect her from feeling vulnerable, but the outcome may be her husband drifting further and further away from the relationship. The previously presented model now looks something like this:

Human organism upon completion of the formative years.	Blocked off internal parts of self-containing valuable resources.

When an alcoholic begins his road to sobriety, he is told to stop drinking, eliminating even more internal territory. Even though giving up alcohol is essential for successful treatment, it also must appear rather ludicrous from the client's perspective. He is already coasting on few internal resources, his survival skills, and now he is told that he has to give up some more in order to survive. This double bind creates what the treatment field has chosen to define as denial and resistance, which has been aptly described by such authors as Jeffrey Shore, John Wallace, and Sharon Wegscheider. Naturally, the uneven path of recovery from alcoholism and concurrent slips are a logical extension of this double bind concept. This also presents a fair explanation regarding the client's "readiness" for treatment. No one can be expected to voluntarily give up survival skills when already feeling inadequate about coping with life. In *Slouching Toward Bethlehem*, Dideon states, "Although to be driven back upon oneself is an uneasy affair at best, it is the one condition necessary to the beginning of self-respect. The dismal fact is that self-respect has nothing to do with approval of others who are, after all, deceived easily enough."

The purpose of NLP is to provide a human being with sufficient internal choices which allow him to move toward well being. With the above in mind then, the intent is not to create new resources, but to assist the client in retrieving his original resources locked away in lost or forgotten parts of himself in order to have access to his own repertoire of internal choices.

What follows then is an NLP technique adapted behaviorally to alcoholism treatment, coupled with several case demonstrations.

SIX-STEP REFRAME

The Six-Step Reframe was one of the original and most versatile NLP techniques. The concept of reframing of course, as in some other school of thoughts is considered a principal treatment modality in Neuro-Linguistic Programming. A previously used example of reframing was the "original intent versus manifested behavior" concept. Reframing as a concept has been used extensively by Satir, Perls, and M. Erickson as well as other proponents of strategic therapy such as Haydy and Watzlawick, as mentioned in this monograph's bibliography. The Six-Step Reframe in this form was developed by Bandler and Grinder, described in their book, *Frogs Into Princes*, and further elaborated in "Reframing." The NLP supposition is that each person is doing the best that he knows how within the internal and external choices available to him. Succinctly stated, the purpose of the Six-Step Reframe is to create more choices. It was designed as a technique that can be used to allow for changes in chronic or recurring behavior, certain habitual responses, etc., all applicable to the treatment of alcoholism. Reframing is a way to change the meaning of a particular stimulus, which in turn changes the way the alcoholic responds to the stimulus. "The meaning that any event has depends upon the frame in which we perceive it."[1] As an example of everyday reframing, a famous television commercial reframe is two little boys not eating cereal because "it is supposed to be good" for them, but when Mikey digs in and obviously enjoys it, the cereal becomes a much desired commodity. Thus, there is no intrinsic value or meaning to a feeling or behavior and human beings therefore, based on old experiences, attribute this meaning on an individual basis. Yeager states:

> The most adaptable of us are those who have the ability to learn all the most important meanings of any given event. These are the people with the most access to their internal resources . . . reframing techniques are a means of taking a . . .

singular interpretation of an event and giving it new, different, or multiple meanings.[2]

Another reframe which basically creates a double bind is an attractive advertisement of an obvious fun couple having a great time smoking and seeing the clear block with the Surgeon General's grim warning printed conspicuously on the ad. "Changing the meaning of a stimulus allows the mind to elicit an additional response previously inhibited by the person's prior interpretation."[3] New behavior is possible by changing the meaning of a stimulus.

Thus, the Six-Step Reframe is one particular adaptation of the general reframing concept. Each step of the Six-Step Reframe may be elaborated on in the work with the individual client. Since the therapist adds choices to the alcoholic's repertoire of behavior, it is important that he model this skill in his own use of flexibility in counseling, carefully staying in rapport with the client and calibrating during each step that the client is obtaining the result that moves him toward his well formed outcome (see chapter of rapport skills). Ron Klein, NLP trainer and director of the American Hypnotherapy Institute in Washington, describes the components of the Six-Step Reframe in his hypnotherapy workbook as follows:[4]

– "Identify the pattern or behavior to be changed." What the therapist asks the alcoholic is simply, in the framework of well formedness conditions, what the client wants and what specifically stops him from getting there at this time (i.e., "I cannot stop drinking because . . . ")
– "Establish communication with the part that generates the behavior." The alcoholic is asked to check if there is a part of him (as opposed to all of him) that is responsible for the drinking behavior. Typically, alcoholism may be defined as a sequential rather than a simultaneous phenomenon (the alcoholic is either in his sober self or in his "drunk" self – whether he is drinking or not) and alcoholism counselors become adept at identifying alcoholics at risk of a relapse as opposed to sober alcoholics. Sequential means that it is impossible to be in both states at the same time. By asking this question, not only does the alcoholic realize that he has parts that are allies in his sobri-

ety, even if there is a part that objects to being sober, but there is also effective use of some of the sorting mechanisms discussed elsewhere in this monograph such as use of dissociation. At this point, sometimes after a little coaxing, the alcoholic will get an internal representation of the part that is responsible for the drinking behavior, generally in the form of an image, but it may also appear as a voice or as a feeling. At this point, the therapist teaches the alcoholic to be very appreciative of any communication this internal part is willing to establish, since the natural tendency of the alcoholic who is in his sober part may be to scold it. The client must understand that the alcoholic part is a component of his survival skills and will only accept changes if it is presented as an invitation to examine additional internal alternatives to the drinking behavior that responds as successfully, or preferably even better to the original needs. Therefore, the next step is to . . .

– "Separate the (original positive) intention (of the drinking behavior) from the (actually manifested) behavior." It is important for the counselor to acknowledge the original intent of that part in the context of the alcoholic's survival skills. The therapist then asks the part, by the client's interpretation of his internal experience if it is willing to cooperate in finding ways for satisfying the original intent. Given the premise of the human organism naturally moving toward well being, the drinking part, when treated with great flexibility will eventually participate in creating more appropriate choices to respond to the original intent.

– "Create alternative behaviors to satisfy the intention." The therapist and alcoholic client may create a number of viable alternatives at this time, or more congruently, the counselor may ask the client if there is another part of him who, at times in his life, has had the capability of being creative, learned, or constructive in some other way. The therapist can ask the alcoholic client to create a second image, of his wise or creative part and discuss examples when this part played an important role in obtaining what the client needed. The image may be visual, auditory, or may be represented by a feeling. The therapist then suggests to the alcoholic that he asks his creative or wise part to come up with three to five new ways of dealing with life other than with the use of alcohol. Some of these ways will appear on a conscious level, others will remain largely unconscious. It is important for the therapist to continually affirm the client, letting him know that whatever he is doing is perfect for him at this time, and to check in with the sober part regularly to keep the alcoholic firmly anchored in the therapist's office doing a reframe with his drinking part.

– The therapist checks with the alcoholic part and asks him to temporarily accept at least one of the new choices, but as many as he wants and to be willing over the next two weeks or so (remember that alcoholics generally sort for "in-time" and that time frames that include a faraway future are not likely to be as successful as those which are largely contained within a measurable present) to test out one or more of these new behaviors as they were designed by the creative or wise part and to generate these behaviors in appropriate contexts when its original intention needs to be fulfilled.

– "Ecological check." The therapist asks the client to check if there are any parts of himself that appear to object to the preceding negotiations and, if not, if he then feels that all of him is willing to support testing new behavioral forms that support the original intention of the drinking behavior.

The following are some demonstrations of treatment of alcoholics or alcoholic systems using Bandler and Grinder's Six-Step Reframe Format as adjusted to alcoholism counseling.

CASE A

An alcoholic woman came to me referred by a psychiatrist. She wanted to stop drinking and had done so several times over the past two years, but she had always returned to drinking alcoholically after ninety to one hundred days of sobriety. What occurred to us was that she had a mechanism for getting sober – she considered ninety days of sobriety the actual test of getting sober—but she had no mechanism for staying sober. We found that the part that was responsible for returning to drinking, for what she had termed "extended slips" in the past, was continuing the behavior because it protected her from failure (by actually failing, which is a frequently occurring paradox). The part of this woman that returned to drinking did not believe that she had the skills to be successful in her profession or in her personal relationships. The part that she chose to design additional ways of protecting her from failure was her adult part and this part generated a number of ways to safeguard the sober person from failing. This client stayed sober one year and then had a slip. When she returned to therapy, it turned out that the part that had created a return to alcoholic behavior in the past had been triggered by the next milestone, the one year sobriety. Adjustments were made within the original Six-Step Reframe, allowing for a great deal of flexibility within the woman's repertoire of internal choices. She has now maintained her sobriety for two years and four months and has learned a second reframe, namely that success is taking risks and that this success is largely not dependent on the outcome of the risk taken. A third important reframe this client integrated was that we were able to use her last slip to obtain information, rather than perceiving it as failure, so that her slip actually assisted her in her continued sobriety. The heart of reframing is to make the distinction between the intention of the behavior—in this case to protect her from failure—and the actual manifested behavior: drinking alcoholically. It is important to remember that, as Bandler states, "Systems work."[5] The difficulty is that the price the human being pays for being successful—in this case drinking alcoholically—becomes too high at some point and that is the time at which alternatives need to be created that are at least as or preferably even more successful in meeting the original intent as the dysfunctional behavior was. Given that the human organism naturally moves toward well being, the therapist can rely on the fact that when drinking alcoholically has become too costly for the individual, he will automatically gravitate toward or choose the alternatives perceived as "most economically" for the human system.

CASE B

A second example involves a woman who had been sober for two years but who had suffered from paralyzing migraines since she got sober. In examining her lifestyle carefully and comparing it to the life she led while abusing alcohol, what became obvious was that since she got sober, she had become a very "good" person, going to AA meetings several times a week, going to church on Sunday, never missing work, and being an excellent spouse and mother. What was missing was the activity the alcoholic part had been responsible for, playing. Since she had connected playing to her alcoholism, she had removed all triggers from her life which in the past would have activated her playful part, but her drinking behavior as well, such as listening to country and western music, buying expensive perfume, etc. Since we now were aware of the positive intent of the drinking behavior, we completed the Six-Step Reframe by separating the established intent—to create playfulness, fun, joy in Micky's life—from the drinking behavior and to have her experience the original triggers followed by fun, disconnected from drinking. Once this client began to recreate joy and fun in her life, the migraines decreased and eventually entirely disappeared.

CASE C

The third example involves a 38-year-old male client who only drank excessively before he had to take trips that involved driving on the highways. He was well aware of the dangers of accidents, losing his license, and a myriad of other problems, not the least of which was his wife's refusal to accompany him on trips. It became evident that this man had been fearful in cars since the time, at age six, he was in the car with his father who, under the influence of alcohol, got into a serious car accident, leaving him handicapped for life. The client vowing never to pick up a drink, found himself under the influence of alcohol each time he had to make a trip. In separating the intent from the manifested behavior in therapy it occurred to him that the drinking behavior had two specific positive purposes. The first one was that alcohol combatted the fear, the second one was that if he were drunk, he could pretend that he was not actually there and could therefore not get into an accident (the paradox again). In completing the Six-Step Reframe, this man designed more than half a dozen ways for satisfying both original intents—he became prolific because he was really excited by his discovery and his ability to finally be in charge of himself in that area of his life—which included agreements with himself to, for a certain time only, drive at 50 mph in the right lane, in daylight hours, with someone who could take over the driving if necessary (his wife was delighted!) and to date he has not picked up another drink, in spite of the fact that he and his wife took a two week vacation driving from New York to Maine and back.

It is important to reiterate here an earlier distinction made between the treatment of alcoholism and other forms of psychotherapy, namely that alcoholism is a sequential illness. What this means is that when an alcoholic is in his drunk or drinking "self," he has a large amount of "amnesia" for his sober goals, and when he is in his sober "self," he frequently cannot believe or understand how he could do some of things he does, how he can jeopardize family, job, etc., for a drink. That is why it is essential to access both parts, the sober as well as the drinking part in doing the intervention. The motivated client, sitting in the therapist's office, is already sober. He is not the one who creates the drinking issues, he is already the therapist's ally. Obviously, however, he is frequently not strong enough to stay in charge of the whole person when triggers appear that elicit the alcoholic part to be in charge. There is much truth to the description many spouses give to their alcoholic husbands and wives, that of the Jekyll and Hyde syndrome. What they are describing is the sequential aspect of alcoholism and any successful intervention needs to take this component into consideration. The above described uses of the original NLP Six-Step Reframe have accommodated for the sequential aspect of alcoholism with the purpose of obtaining an appropriate integration of the two parts as the end result. It is important to bear in mind that the purpose is indeed appropriate integration, not elimination of the alcoholic part. The client can never "give up" any part—no human being can—since drinking alcoholically has become part of his survival skills. Given, however, more efficient usage of survival skills coupled with increased access to internal resources, the alcoholic part can find additional ways of having the needs of the client met, other than by drinking behavior. At that point, this part can actually integrate with the sober part of the individual, creating a far firmer base for continued sobriety.

SUMMARY AND CONCLUSION

The technique called Six-Step Reframe exemplifies some of the most significant tenets of NLP, the creation and behavioral installment of an internal repertoire of choices to deal effectively with presenting life events, the belief that individuals have all the resources they need to lead satisfying lives, that the therapist's primary job is to assist the client in accessing these internal resources and that all behavior, no matter how bizarre, makes sense in the context in which it was originated. It furthermore demonstrates that there is a positive connotation to be found to all dysfunctional behavior and that this connotation becomes the pivotal point for turning present negative behavior around by providing an internal repertoire of choices that responds more appropriately to these original needs. Finally given the opportunity, the human organism moves toward well being and this opportunity is created by generating the previously discussed internal alternatives and choices. People create their beliefs about life out of their internal representations of reality. I would like to end this chapter with a short metaphor told by a client.

> A Zen student is told that some high officials are coming to visit his temple and the student immediately set about cleaning up the garden. Grass was trimmed to only grow where it was supposed to, the pebbles were confined to the paths, there were no weeds in sight, and all fallen blossoms had been cleaned up. Anxiously peering over the temple wall, he saw a friend from a neighboring temple, also a student in Zen Buddhism. He called the friend into the garden and in a worried

voice asked, "Do you think my garden is perfect?" His friend took a stick, moved some of the earth onto the path, hit some of the trees so that some blossoms and leaves gently floated to the ground, moved some of the pebbles outside of the path and then looked up and smilingly said, "Now it is perfect."

REFERENCES

1. Bandler, R. and J. Grinder, Reframing, p. 1.
2. Yeager, J. Thinking About Thinking With NLP, p. 69, 170.
3. ENLPI, unpublished conference literature, 1984.
4. Washington Hypnotherapy Training Institute, unpublished conference literature, 1985.
5. Bandler, R. and J. Grinder, *Frogs Into Princes*, p. 138.

Chapter 7

Cognitive-Perceptual Reconstruction in the Treatment of Alcoholism

James O. Henman PhD
Sonia M. Henman, MS

The impact of alcoholism on our lives has become increasingly clear in recent years. The cost to the alcoholics, their families and society as a whole is staggering. Recent statistics indicate that approximately one family in six in nearly 30 million men, women and children in our country are directly affected by this disease (Black, 1981). The approaches used to treat this tragic problem have been varied and have been less supportive of one another than would be most helpful for those struggling with this disease. Self-help groups, using the Twelve Step model of Alcoholics Anonymous, Al-Anon and Adult Children of Alcoholics, contend that their structure and support for those affected by this disease is the primary path to recovery. Because of a subtle and sometimes overt mistrust of psychotherapy, members involved in these programs may be discouraged by other members from seeking additional support in therapy (Brown, 1985). The lack of specific training in alcoholism for many therapists has contributed to this reaction. Traditional psychotherapists, although not being very successful in treating alcoholism themselves, sometimes have difficulty accepting and supporting certain elements of the Anonymous approach, e.g., the acceptance of powerlessness over alcohol, surrendering to a Higher Power, the strong emphasis on identifying oneself as an alcoholic, and the encouragement of dependency on the group and its principles (Bean, 1975; Beckman, 1980; Leach and Norris, 1977). The philosophical differences in attitude and emphasis between these two groups have been a source of confusion for many affected by alcoholism, and tend to undermine cooperation between these two potential sources of help. It is our experience that the treatment of alcoholism often requires a comprehensive, multi-faceted and integrated intervention. We have found that effective recovery is often facilitated by a close working relationship between the person affected by the disease and a psychotherapist, as well as active involvement in "Twelve Step Programs." We have also found it necessary to combine and integrate a number of different psychotherapeutic approaches into a process we term Cognitive Perceptual Reconstruction (Henman, 1987).

Cognitive-Perceptual Reconstruction (CPR) has its roots in Cognitive Behavior Modification, Client-Centered Therapy, Family Systems Theory, Analytic Psychotherapy, the hypnotic patterns of Milton H. Erickson, Neuro-Linguistic Programming, the Twelve Step Anonymous Programs, and the model of change presented in the Christian Gospel. CPR combines and integrates these varied approaches into a unifying philosophy and style of intervention. Rather than simply employing a set of intervention techniques, CPR embodies a therapeutic attitude about recovery that creates an atmosphere within which change is a natural consequence.

The goals of CPR are to facilitate recovery by: (1) developing a loving, respectful New Program Adult (NP Adult) who mediates between the various aspects of the client's personality and creates a safe atmosphere for growth and change; (2) teaching the client to perceive both internal and external events more accurately by becoming aware of underlying presuppositions which limit perceptual choices; (3) teaching the client more functional interpersonal skills and (4) initiating an attitude within the client that accepts recovery as a lifetime process.

At the heart of CPR is a set of principles, the first of which is the belief in the intrinsic value of mutual respect. This respect needs to be applied in relating to oneself as well as to others and thus becomes a structure which gives direction and guidance in daily living. The second principle is the belief that there must be an accepting relationship between the conscious mind of the client and the unconscious parts of self that have been dissociated in the process of growing up in an unsafe environment. Recovery requires a change of attitude from self-rejecting shame to forgiveness of self and others. This shift allows the experiencing of honest feelings of regret for past pain. The third principle is the belief in the Twelve Step concept of a loving Higher Power as each person understands that Higher Power to be. This belief assumes a resource greater than self, which cares about each individual personally. It holds that each person has significant value and therefore the choices made during life have impact in some greater reality. These three principles form the core of what we call "New Program."

In CPR the therapist actively explores and reframes the "Old Program" which is currently limiting the client. This "Old Program" includes the client's underlying assumptions, beliefs, attitudes, perceptual filters, internal dialogue, and unconscious patterns of processing information. While the client is treated with unconditional respect by the therapist, this "Old Program" is challenged, reframed and altered to be more compatible with a healthy life style. CPR utilizes the interactive process between the therapist and client, and this process becomes a model for a "New Program Adult." The NP Adult learns to relate to the disconnected parts of self as well as the outside world with an attitude of respect. Recovery is the process of progressively internalizing this NP Adult.

An important element of the therapeutic process is changing the person's attitude toward "undesirable" feelings. Rather than responding to these feelings as if they were a threat to be blocked and avoided, the underlying communicative value of the feelings is emphasized. The client is taught to utilize these feelings as a vehicle for making loving, respectful contact with the disconnected parts of self and it is primarily through this reconnection that healing is facilitated.

THE SOCIAL CONTEXT OF ALCOHOLISM AND A LOOK AT THE DISEASE

The disease of alcoholism can best be understood in the light of present cultural attitudes and beliefs. Our society is permeated with many subtle messages which contribute to the problem of alcoholism. There is an underlying fear of pain and a worship of comfort. Advertisements tell us that if we have pain we should "take an aspirin" and if we can't sleep we should "take Sominex." We are told that we shouldn't "let them see us sweat" because we should be calm and confident at all times. We are told that if we want to be more popular, we need to know how to order the right beer; sex and friendship are available at our nearest tavern. We must get what we want when we want it, or it is "awful." Mass media makes it easy to confuse needs and wants. New is better. We shouldn't have to work hard at relationships. Things and other people should make us feel good. We should feel happy and peaceful at all times, or there is something terribly wrong. These, and other messages affect our expectations and become the background for us to view ourselves and our lives. Children are particularly affected by this programming, and Adult Children of Dysfunction are no exception. Within this social context, the disease of alcoholism is experienced by alcoholics, their co-dependent partners, and children who grow up in this toxic environment.

The Alcoholic

Much has been written about the changes which take place in alcoholics as the disease progresses (Jellinek, 1960; Polich et al., 1981; Royce, 1981). These researchers and others have found a number of psychological and biological changes which appear to be associated with alcoholism. There is growing evidence of a relationship between alcoholic drinking and a reduction in neuro-transmitter levels of dopamine, serotonin and norepinephrine (Blum & Trachtenberg, 1987). Ethanol has the capacity to displace enkephalins and endorphins at binding sites which decrease these levels in the brain and pituitary, thus resulting in alcohol craving (Blum & Topel, 1986). At the psychological level there has developed a recognizable cluster of personality traits associated with alcoholism, including a low tolerance for stress, feelings of inadequacy, impaired impulse control, isolation and a negative image of self.

There seems to be agreement that at a point in the progression of the disease, people cross into alcohol addiction. It is at this time that alcohol becomes the organizing core around which everything else in the alcoholic's life must relate. When this happens, alcoholics can no longer predict their behavior while drinking, or even whether or not they will drink. Dr. Stephanie Brown (1985) has explored these developmental changes in cognition which lead to "alcoholic thinking." She states that these changes refer "not only to rationalization, denial and frame of mind, but also to character traits that frequently accompany drinking. These include grandiosity, omnipotence and low frustration tolerance." (Brown, 1988, pp. 97). These traits appear to be directly associated with the addictive process rather than with the individual's personality prior to establishing this abusive cycle.

As alcohol becomes more dominant, the need to deny these changes becomes greater. It appears that there is an interaction between physiological changes and psychological defenses which creates emotional immaturity, self-centeredness and irresponsibility. Alcoholism becomes a thought disorder as well as an addiction to alcohol.

These qualities would accurately describe the primary defenses and interpersonal style typical of normal development in the first three years of life. We have found it useful to characterize the addictive part of self as a two-year-old child. The widespread appreciation of the "terrible twos" stage of human development gives alcoholics a new way of understanding what is happening inside. Alcoholics increasingly utilize the psychological defenses of denial, undoing, isolation, and rationalization to keep from facing reality. This progressive use of these early defenses forms the two-year-old who begins to "drive the bus" and create havoc for all concerned. As the disease develops, the two-year-old becomes predominant while the adult influence atrophies with disuse. When fully formed, the two-year-old becomes a permanent part of the alcoholic's personality. The use of alcohol and other drugs strengthens the power of the two-year-old and at the same time weakens the adult. The primary focus of therapeutic intervention in CPR is to develop healthy supervision for the two-year-old by the NP Adult.

ADULT CHILDREN OF ALCOHOLICS AND CO-DEPENDENT PARTNERS

The impact of growing up in a world dominated by a two-year-old parent, or being married to that same two-year-old, has profound effects. The emotional climate of the home becomes progressively dictated by alcohol. Therapist Claudia Black (1981) described the family rules in an alcoholic home as "don't talk," "don't trust," and "don't feel." Author Janet Woititz (1983, 1985) has summarized a number of characteristics of people who grow up affected by another's alcoholism. These people spend a lifetime looking for normalcy; they are constantly seeking approval and affirmation; they judge themselves without mercy; and they have a great difficulty with intimate relationships. Children growing up in environments where it is unsafe to be a child often learn to act in ways which are beyond their developmental age. They become "adults" as children and often function as "children" in adult life. This drive to get the needed reactions and support from their parents leads them to reject and dissociate significant aspects of themselves. John Bradshaw (1988) has coined the term "toxic shame" to describe the rejection of self that is so common with Adult Children of Dysfunction. The degree of dysfunction in Adult Children of Dysfunction is proportional to the amount of self currently contaminated by the shame associated with past events and decisions.

The survival strategy of Adult Children of Dysfunction varies depending on a number of factors, including birth order, sex, intrinsic personality predisposition, etc. Some Adult Children of Dysfunction adopt very rigid, over-controlling, hyper-responsible postures toward the world. These "little parents" try to manage their fear and anxiety by being perfectly on top of everything. Their drive for perfect control always fails, and they tend to turn this failure into self-rejection. Other Adult Children of Dysfunction take on all the emotional pain and blame for everything that goes wrong, either with themselves or those around them. They assume the posture of an "emotional sponge," filling the empty place left by their self-rejection. Some Adult Children of Dysfunction become "identified patients" and take on the burden of shifting the focus of attention in the family onto themselves and away from the problems caused by the alcoholic. Some Adult Children of Dysfunction identify so closely with the alcoholic parent that they take on the alcoholic's dysfunctional patterns. Still other Adult Children of Dysfunction learn to become "chameleons" and opt for the safety of invisibility. These survival strategies are not mutually exclusive.

There is also a significant impact on the adult partners of alcoholics. These partners often demonstrate the dynamics of co-dependency which have begun to receive growing attention (Beattie, 1987; Schaef, 1986). The co-dependent partners, who are usually Adult Children of Dysfunction, become progressively obsessed with the alcoholic's drinking and with trying to control the destructive behavior of the two-year-old in the alcoholics. As the alcoholics become increasingly less responsible for what is happening in the family, the full pressure falls onto the co-dependent partners. These partners are often unconsciously drawn to the familiarity of this situation, even though they have the feelings that result from it. Their "Inner Child" knows the rules of this type of environment and knows that survival is possible. The process of socializing women to gain their sense of identity and self-esteem from their male partners can also add to this problem. The demands to continue in the pathological relationship, whether religious, financial or emotional, lead the co-dependent partners to feel trapped. This growing preoccupation with the alcoholic causes the co-dependent partners to lose more and more of self as the disease progresses. If they can't control the alcoholic, their sense of self is at risk. It literally becomes a life and death struggle.

One co-dependent described herself as a structure with many rooms. A few of the rooms were nicely furnished, and the outside world was allowed to see these rooms. There were many others rooms that were sparsely furnished or totally empty. She felt tremendous shame and fear that the rest of the world would find out about her lack of furnishings and reject her. She was therefore desperately looking for her partner to supply the needed furnishings for these other rooms to become complete. This was something her alcoholic partner could never successfully do for her, and as a result she experienced progressively more frustration, resentment, and despair.

THEORETICAL ASSUMPTIONS OF COGNITIVE-PERCEPTUAL RECONSTRUCTION

In understanding and treating the disease of alcoholism, we have found a number of important dynamic processes and concepts useful. Although many different psychological defense mechanisms are active in alcoholism, the process of dissociation has particularly significant implications. Dissociation involves the rejection or disconnection of a part of self. This disconnection includes the inner feeling of shame as well as any other feelings of pain associated with the events at the time of dissociation. Although there are important events occurring throughout life, we have found that most Adult Children of Dysfunction fixate at a few developmentally critical ages. It is these fixated points we call the "children within." These Inner Children retain their original perceptual filters, developmental resources, and cognitive styles which become frozen in the timeless repository of the unconscious mind. They also retain the decisions they made about themselves and their world at the time of the fixation event. One of the common decisions centers around their perception of personal power. They learn over and over they cannot change their environment or control the drinking. These repeated experiences of "learned helplessness" lead to feelings of powerlessness and despair.

The concept of "state dependent learning" has direct implications on the dynamics of dissociation and regression. We have found that contact with one specific fixated "Inner Child" does not necessarily generalize to other fixated ages. The role of the NP (New Program, as was defined on p. 106) Adult remains the same with all rejected parts of self, whether aged three, six, ten or twenty-four. These different ages usually have specific issues, styles and decisions which need to be dealt with as contact develops. The NP Adult is taught to supply the needed resources for each dissociated part.

Either internal or external events can trigger a regression in Adult Children of Dysfunction which brings the dissociated Inner Child, with the original feelings of powerlessness and despair, to the surface. When this regression happens, the individuals actually become the "child within" and lose access to their adult resources. It is for this reason that the term "over reaction" can be misleading. What may be an over reaction for an adult may be developmentally appropriate for a young child. How many six-year-olds do you know who can drive a car, hold down a full-time job, raise a family, and deal with the intricacies of marriage? An Adult Child of Dysfunction may take a college course as a 35-year-old woman, but when it comes time to take a test may suddenly regress back to a nine-year-old little girl. She begins to feel the pain associated with her alcoholic father browbeating her for not getting all of her spelling words perfect. These feelings of fear, anger and powerlessness become superimposed on the current test situation in the college classroom, greatly inhibiting performance. The woman feels inadequate and stupid and when she tries to function from a regressed state, these feelings become a self-fulfilling prophecy. Nine-year-olds do not perform as well as thirty-five-year olds on a college test.

When clients are in Old Program, if often means they have abandoned the "child" to deal with the current situation. In the previous example, the therapist would confront the woman in a respectful way for having abandoned her little nine-year-old girl to do an adult's job. Then the therapist would walk through the situation with the NP Adult giving needed skills, reframing cognitions and perceptions, and adding resources where necessary. In this way, the NP Adult can make contact with that nine-year-old and comfort and reassure her directly. This allows clients to have access to the resources of New Program. The therapist serves as a model, coach, traffic cop, and translater in this process.

The therapist and clients can recognize when regression is happening by subtle changes in the clients' non-verbal communication. The clients' tone of voice and intonation become more child-like. Facial expressions change to give the impression of youth. Their perceptions are altered, i.e., they feel smaller and more powerless. The clients may have the feeling of being a fake when exercising whatever competence they may actually have. They report a fear of being "discovered," "found out," or "caught." There tends to be cognitive developmental signs such as a rigid, concrete style of thinking (e.g., things are either black or white), signs of "magical thinking," and a feeling of not being able to survive on their own. This would be appropriate if they were in fact five or six years of age, but is a clear distortion of reality as an adult.

It is important for the therapist to appreciate the differences in style and approach between surviving and healthy living. The decisions that would be functional for a child growing up in a chaotic alcoholic environment become dysfunctional in a healthy relationship. Without this understanding, it would be easy to judge these early decisions as bad or wrong. The fact is these decisions were the best ones available to the child at that time, given his/her resources and developmental maturity. Reframing the frozen scenes to include these distinctions is an important part of the healing process. Acknowledging these differences to the client and creating a "no fault" context for learning New Program reduces resistances to change, and makes dealing with denial much easier. It needs to be emphasized throughout treatment that change is a gradual process of steps forward and steps backward. The client is taught to celebrate even small steps forward and to view steps backward as opportunities to learn. Recovery is a lifetime commitment to this learning process.

CPR combines conscious and unconscious interventions in therapy. The hypnotic patterns of Milton H. Erickson and the tools of Neuro-Linguistic Programming are utilized to affect the unconscious. At the same time, there is a lot of conscious teaching of skills and attitudes in helping the client learn to apply New Program. The client is taught to become aware of internal dialogue and how to challenge dysfunctional messages. The tone and underlying assumptions of the dialogue have as much impact as the words. We have coined the term "Commentator" to represent the various elements of internal dialogue. It is important to understand that the Commentator was formed in a dysfunctional environment in the process of growing up. In that original setting the harsh and invalidating messages had survival value. The child learned to internalize parental actions and the Commentator would anticipate parental messages before they would actually be given. This allowed the child to avoid some of the pain of receiving the messages directly from the parent. The Commentator can activate regression by reproducing these familiar messages. Recovery involves having the NP Adult progressively take on more of the Commentator function.

The client often strongly resists re-experiencing painful scenes from the past. Splitting the "part of self" which is most deeply experiencing these feelings from the rest of the client allows the feelings to be split as well. Since the Child is already experiencing the feelings associated with the original scene, the NP Adult does not need to feel the same original feelings.

There is a difference between breaking your arm and having someone you love break an arm. In the first instance the primary pain is focused on the physical sensation in the arm. In the second instance the feelings may run the gamut from sympathy or empathy, to guilt that somehow you should have prevented it, to anger at the loved one for getting hurt, to feeling responsible in some way, etc.

Therapy can take advantage of this difference by coaching the client *how* to enter the painful scene. The NP Adult can bring the compassion, respect, validation, and nurturing into the scene. With these new resources the "child within" can experience the original scene in a new, healthier way. The NP Adult makes it possible for the child to shift from the shameful rejection of self to the more accurate feeling of regret that the event ever happened. This shift advances the healing process.

APPLICATION OF COGNITIVE-PERCEPTUAL RECONSTRUCTION

Treatment of the Alcoholic

The transition from active alcoholic drinking into recovery is a rocky and stressful process, requiring a great deal of support and structure (Brown, 1985). We have found that many alcoholics need the safety and concentrated help of a 28-day in-patient program during the initial shift from drinking to sobriety. These programs can lay the seeds of recovery and provide a drug-free environment to begin practicing "New Program." One of the most important shifts necessary during this early transition is the recognition and acceptance that the alcoholic is powerless over alcohol or any other drug that would weaken the adult supervision and increase the power of the two-year-old. There is a tremendous amount of information about the disease which needs to be learned by the alcoholic and his/her family. During this time, the alcoholic and the family need to be introduced to the resources available through A.A. and Al-Anon. We have found that those who begin to actively work the Twelve Step program during this transitional period have a much higher rate of success.

The key to recovery with the alcoholic is the question of responsibility. The application of the two-year-old model of addiction speaks to the heart of responsibility. Once the alcoholic accepts that there is an addictive part of self that functions like a two-year-old, the question of supervision is a logical next step. Most alcoholics have seen, or been around a two-year-old child at some time in their lives. The therapist challenges them to consider whether they would be willing to leave such a child unattended to do whatever that child wanted. Most alcoholics would not think of doing such a thing. This example leads into the question of who is going to supervise the two-year-old addict *inside*. This immediately brings up the issue of sobriety because alcohol and other mind-altering drugs have two effects simultaneously: they weaken the adult and fortify the two-year-old. It is for this reason that New Program strongly supports sobriety; it is not respectful to leave a two-year-old unsupervised.

The model also has an effect on denial. Most alcoholics feel such guilt and shame for the damage they have done while drinking that these feelings are overwhelming. With this model, the real villain or culprit is the lack of supervision. Obviously, the two-year-old is developmentally unable to be held responsible for his/her actions. We will often ask alcoholics the following questions: Who would be responsible if a two-year-old was left alone at home for the evening and, while unattended, broke several expensive things around the house by accident? Would it be the child, the parents or the lack of adequate supervision? Should the child be hated and rejected? Recovering alcoholics are taught that they can most directly deal with the remorse about pain caused from past drinking by committing themselves to developing a healthy, supervisorial, parenting relationship with the two-year-old in the present. The emphasis is on turning self-rejecting shame into remorse, and then change. Alcoholics are taught to recognize when the two-year-old is trying to take charge. We believe what has been termed "dry drunk" during sobriety is often actually the two-year-old acting up. The NP Adult is taught to reframe the craving to drink as a tangible sign of loving the two-year-old enough to say "no."

Jerry, a forty-seven-year-old alcoholic-poly-drug abuser with one hundred days of sobriety, was having significant difficulty maintaining his sobriety. The desire to drink was constantly on his mind, and he had had three near relapses in the prior two weeks.

The following is an excerpt of this therapy session:

Jerry: "I can't help it doc. Everything I see makes me think about getting high. I feel so bored and empty. If it weren't for this constant fear of drinking, I wouldn't be feeling anything at all."

Therapist: "Jerry, it seems as if you are using a tremendous amount of energy in NOT drinking. All you seem to be thinking about is not relapsing, and fighting to try to ignore the urge to drink."

Jerry: "Of course! I go to meetings all the time, I never feel safe. I know that if I have another drink I am going to die."

Therapist: "Jerry, do you remember me talking about the two-year-old addictive part of you when you were going through the program?"

Jerry: "Yeah, now that you mention it, but I had forgotten all about that. I have been so busy trying not to drink, that I guess I forgot a lot of things from the programs."

Therapist: "Well Jerry, it is real easy to do, and what is important is to allow yourself to remember now, and to begin to use the tools you have learned now that you remember. Take a moment . . . here in the safety of my office . . . to let yourself really feel the urge to drink, to really experience what is going on inside. Allow those feelings to float up to an image of that two-year-old Jerry, and just notice how big he seems as you begin to look at him."

Jerry: "Shit, he seems huge!"

Therapist: "Look again Jerry. Allow yourself to see him for the two-year-old he really is. Don't be confused by the intensity of his tantrum. You need to love him enough to say *NO* in a caring and respectful way."

Jerry: "He seems so small now. How can he have so much power? I mean, I really feel out of control and scared so much of the time."

Therapist: "Of course you do Jerry. What is happening inside is that you forgot to parent little Jerry, and so you became him. The adult was able to get you to meetings, but that is as far as he went. Give yourself credit for that much. Celebrate the fact that you have maintained your sobriety. It is natural for a two-year-old to feel overwhelmed when he doesn't have an adult to take care of him. Is it O.K. for us to do it in an easier way?"

Jerry: "Sure!"

Therapist: "I want you to keep that two-year-old with you every where you go this week. Take him to the meetings with you, take him to work with you, take him with you when you go to the bathroom. I want you to understand he is going to tantrum, and that is fine. What is important is for you to remember that you are a hell of a lot bigger than he is, and can protect him and yourself as you ride out the tantrums."

Jerry: "I've got to remember that he is a little kid."

Therapist: "That's right Jerry, and the more loving, firm and consistent you can be with him, the easier it will become. He needs to learn that he can trust you to be there, and to keep the limits consistent and predictable. It is also important to begin saying YES to healthy things. Let yourself begin to have some fun with him in between the tantrums."

Although the majority of alcoholics are Adult Children of Dysfunction, the primary focus of treatment in therapy during the first year of sobriety is learning to create and develop a healthy, loving relationship with the two-year-old. The NP Adult's first order of business is keeping a chemically-free environment in which to learn "New Program" and the "Twelve Steps." Other Adult Child of Dysfunction issues are addressed only when they threaten ongoing sobriety. We have found this limited focus during the fragile transition allows the alcoholics to begin learning the skills and attitudes which will generalize to other Adult Child of Dysfunction issues as sobriety becomes more stable. There are enough changes to go through during the first year without digging up material. The consequences of having allowed the two-year-old to be in charge while drinking begin to surface during this time. Damaged relationships demand attention, and emotions which were previously medicated with alcohol flood into awareness. The alcoholics usually do not have the skills to deal with these pressures. The role of the therapist, in conjunction with A.A. and Al-Anon, is to provide coaching and a new way to approach these problems. The alcoholics, as well as the family, often develop significant dependency on the therapist and the Twelve Step programs during this transition period. One sign of healthy movement into recovery is a gradual reduction of this dependency.

TREATMENT OF ADULT CHILDREN OF DYSFUNCTION AND CO-DEPENDENTS

The therapeutic approach of CPR should not be limited to the alcoholic, but rather extended to facilitate the recovery of those in the alcoholic environment as well. It is important for Adult Children of Dysfunction and co-dependent partners to re-experience the original scenes in which dissociation has taken place. They need to make loving contact with their "Inner Children" in order for healing to occur. The key distinction is *how* the process of re-experiencing will be approached in therapy. CPR encourages clients to use feelings of shame and other strong emotions to help bring these scenes into focus. As clients are experiencing these painful feelings more fully in the present, they are given the suggestion to allow their feelings to float up into images and to begin to *see* what is being felt. They are also encouraged to hear what the "commentator" is saying inside as the feelings are intensifying. The suggestion is given that they may begin to notice scenes from the past and are encouraged to allow their unconscious minds to select a scene in which these feelings were particularly intense. They are then asked to see themselves in the scene as they were at that time.

The clients are then encouraged to watch the scene and tell their therapist what they see and how they feel about themselves in the scene. The clients will often describe feelings of shame and rejection toward the child in the image. The therapist must challenge these feelings by reframing the clients' perceptions of themselves in the scene and changing the tone, attitude and content of their internal dialogue. The therapist is a strong advocate of treating the Inner Children with respect during this process. Healing cannot begin until this change of heart from rejection to acceptance takes place. The therapist uses a very warm, nurturing tone and attitude while reframing these scenes.

Mary is a thirty-two-year old single parent with three children. She has worked hard professionally to achieve a position of responsibility in the company where she works. Mary is an Adult Child of Dysfunction with an alcoholic father and an extremely co-dependent mother. She came into therapy after experiencing a series of disabling panic attacks at work. Her new supervisor was a very abrasive fifty-year-old man who would explode at Mary for the slightest error.

The following is a brief excerpt of a therapy session:

Mary: "I felt like I was going to die. One minute my boss was yelling at men, and the next minute my heart was beating out of my chest. I felt like I couldn't breathe, like I was going to suffocate. The room began to close in, and I was sure I was going to faint. It was awful."

Therapist: "As you are telling me about this, it seems as though you are beginning to re-experience those feelings right now as we talk."

Mary: "Yeah, it's not as strong . . . I can't stand it!"

Therapist: "You seem to be trying to push it back down."

Mary: "Of course! I don't want to feel that again."

Therapist: "I am going to ask you to do something that may sound strange, Mary, but it is very important for us to be able to hear and see what the anxiety is trying to communicate to you. . . . Allow yourself to begin to relax into the feelings of growing anxiety. You don't have to be afraid of being afraid. We will go into the feeling together. I am right here with you, and you are safe here in my office. Just move toward the feelings, allow them to intensify and build, to grow stronger with each breath. . . . If you were to give an age to how you are feeling right now, what age would you give yourself?"

Mary: "I don't know. I have never thought about it in that way."

Therapist: "That's O.K. Just allow yourself to pick the first age that comes into your mind. It doesn't have to be right."

Mary: "This sounds strange, but I feel around five-years-old. God, that was a terrible time" (Mary begins to cry). My father had lost his job because of his drinking, and was mad all of the time. He would yell and scream for no reason, and sometimes he would hit me" (Mary sobs).

Therapist: "Allow yourself to see little Mary, five-years-old, afraid to do anything wrong, never knowing what will set Dad off.

See her there in front of you now. See the pain in her face, and notice how you feel about her."

Mary: "Why did she have to be so weak? (angry tone). She looks so ugly with her puffy eyes and red nose."

Therapist: "She is only five-years-old. She has every right to be afraid. Being afraid shows she is a smart little girl. Allow yourself to see her more accurately with the compassion she deserves. Someone like you to protect her from Dad, to nurture her, to help turn her shame into sadness that her Dad has a disease, that her Dad's problem is not her fault, that she cannot control her Dad's drinking. Reach out to her with the love and support she so desperately needs. Forgive her for being five-years-old. Allow yourself to reach out and hold her, to cry with her so that she doesn't have to cry alone."

Mary was taught to recognize when she began to regress back to that little girl. She was taught to see the little girl, to comfort her, rather than becoming the little girl and drowning in anxiety.

Guided imagery and role-playing can be helpful in this process when used with the hypnotic patterns of Milton H. Erickson to deepen the experience. The goal of the intervention is to access the NP Adult in the clients, and have him/her enter the scene with the child. The NP Adult can teach the child to understand the difference between shame and regret. This difference between rejection of self and feeling the pain in the scene allows the NP Adult to support the child through the painful experience. The NP Adult can be there for the child as the child feels the pain of regret, along with any other painful feelings that might be present. The feelings of unconditional acceptance for the child which the NP Adult brings to the scene, begin to address the self-rejecting feelings of shame which are so devastating for the child. At the heart of this process is the forgiveness of the child for being imperfect and lacking power. The NP Adult must be able to forgive the child before the child can forgive self.

The goal with Adult Children of Dysfunction and Co-dependent partners is to begin a nurturing relationship between the NP Adult and the disconnected parts of self. As clients begin to internalize these New Program perceptions and ways of thinking, they begin to claim back lost personal territory which has been frozen in the shadow of shame. The clients are taught to look accurately at things without having judgmental, self-rejecting reactions. When something is undesirable, or if regret is involved, the clients are coached how to begin the process of change as it relates to that specific situation. We have found that feelings of overwhelming shame prevent change. The feelings of regret can become the source of motivation to do something different. There are times when they cannot change something, and at these times they need to accept that there are limits to their power and look for ways to influence the circumstances in any small way possible. What they cannot change, they need to turn over to their Higher Power. The belief in a Loving Higher Power becomes an ongoing resource for clients to draw on in the development and strengthening of their NP Adult. If there is nothing greater than self, and if there is no loving source and meaning to life, then it is easy to feel crushed by past pain.

The therapist combines unconditional positive regard for the Adult Children of Dysfunction and Co-dependent partners, with a very active, observational style of confronting. This style simply presents the clients' situations in a low-keyed, matter of fact tone of voice. The emphasis is on change and growth rather than blaming or understanding "why" something happened. The therapist reframes the clients' perceptions of the past so that it can be experienced emotionally in different ways. The tone of voice of the therapist is very important in this process because the unconscious will respond fairly directly to the tone, tempo and rhythm of the voice.

The therapist can use metaphors to translate the processes of change into the persons' own language. For example, if clients are mechanics, the therapist may talk about an engine and how an engine needs to have an overhaul. They may be told that from time to time there will need to be an oil change and lube. Plumbers may be told that they will need to clean out their pipes before the water can flow properly. Gardeners are shown the importance of weeding and preparing the soil properly before planting. They are also reminded that it takes time for the seeds to germinate into healthy plants. Using word pictures in this way can help them feel safe with the therapy process and begin to perceive that change/growth is an ongoing process. They can accept that they may occasionally need some assistance to get back on track in New Program.

COGNITIVE-PERCEPTUAL RECONSTRUCTION IN ONGOING RECOVERY

The goals of CPR can be distilled down to the establishment and ongoing development of an NP Adult in those who have been affected by the disease of alcoholism. This resource, in conjunction with the continuing support of Twelve Step group meetings, allows the alcoholics, the co-dependent partners, and the Adult Children of Dysfunction to enter a lifetime process of recovery. The NP Adult literally reparents the wounded parts of self with the beliefs, attitudes and skills of New Program. After the initial learning period, the role of the therapist becomes one of supporting the NP Adult in this reparenting process. The frequency and nature of sessions reflects this transition. At first, clients are usually seen on a weekly basis, but as the NP Adult becomes stronger, the period of time between sessions is extended. Many clients find CPR groups helpful during this consolidation period. The opportunity to practice sharing their "private selves" with others who are also struggling with their own recovery is very beneficial at many levels. New Program will never be mastered perfectly. Healthy recovery is the process of enjoying the journey.

REFERENCES

Bean, M. Alcoholics Anonymous I. *Psychiatric Annals*, 1975, *5 (2)*, 7-61.

Beattie, M. *Co-dependents No More*. Center City, MN: Hazelden, 1987.

Beckman, L. An attributional analysis of A. A. *Journal of Studies on Alcohol*, 1980, *41 (7)*, 714-726.

Black, C. *It Will Never Happen To Me*. Denver, CO: M. A. C., 1981.

Blum, K. & Topel, H. Opioid peptides and alcoholism: genetic deficiency and chemical management. *Functional Neurology*, 1986, *1*, 71-79.

Blum, K. & Trachtenberg, M. C. Addicts may lack some neurotransmitters. *The U. S. Journal*, 1987, July, 16.

Bradshaw, J. *Bradshaw on: the family*. Pompano Beach, FL: Health Communications, Inc., 1988.

Brown, S. *Treating the alcoholic, a developmental model of recovery*. New York: John Wiley & Sons, 1985.

Henman, J. O. Conscious competence and other paradoxes for adult children. *Focus*, 1987, July/August.

Jellinek, E. M. *The disease concept of alcoholism*. New Haven, CT: Colleges and Universities Press, 1960.

Leach, B. & Norris, J. L. Factors in the development of Alcoholics Anonymous. In B. Kissin & H. Begleiter (Eds.), *The biology of alcoholism. Treatment and rehabilitation of the chronic alcoholic*, (vol. 5). New York: Plenum Press, 1977, 441-543.

Polich, J. M., Armor, D. J., & Braiker, H. B. *The course of alcoholism: Four years after treatment*. New York: Wiley Interscience, 1981.

Royce, J. E. *Alcohol problems and alcoholism*. New York: Free Press, 1981.

Schaef, A. W. *Co-dependence, misunderstood-mistreated*. San Francisco: Harper & Row, 1986.

Woititz, J. G. *Adult Children of alcoholics*. Pompano Beach, FL: Health Communications, Inc., 1983.

Woititz, J. G. *Struggle for . . . intimacy*. Pompano Beach, FL: Health Communications, Inc., 1985.

Chapter 8

Are You the Product of My Misunderstanding? or The Role of Sorting Mechanisms and Basic Human Programs in the Treatment of Alcoholism

Chelly M. Sterman, MSW, ABECSW, CAC

INTRODUCTION

In accordance with some basic human standards involving ecology and strength in personal identity, Neuro-Linguistic Programming (NLP) has developed some clear methodology. The purpose of this methodology is to create a set of skills and strategies a counselor may choose to use as part of his repertoire to increase the number of clients he can meet within their model of the world and connect to their internal resources. The purpose of NLP is not to replace what works within the counselor's set of skills and strategies, but to add to his repertoire to create the highest level of flexibility for the counselor in a therapeutic situation. This supports their awareness of their model of the world, their internal interpretation of their particular human experience and their needs in their personal journey toward well-being. Individuals may share an experience, but their interpretation will match their internal model of the world. For instance, police reports taken from onlookers at the sight of an accident are known to be widely divergent and depend to a large extent on the viewpoint of the onlooker rather than the actual occurrence (i.e., opinions about women drivers, drivers of expensive cars, teenage drivers, "speeding," etc.). Thus, personal interpretation of the experience in significant ways affects the outcomes the therapist obtains in working with alcoholic systems, which frequently contributes to the alcoholic population described as being difficult, complicated, even unrewarding to work with. NLP's contribution here consists of the additional strategies to the counselor's repertoire which allow him to accurately measure, calibrate, which standards the alcoholic measures realities with and to which basic human program he does or does not have access. Thus, the intent of this chapter is to further provide what NLP calls "requisite variety," the necessary internalized skills, techniques, strategies, and methods to meet the needs of the alcoholic population. The intent is to add to the counselor's flexibility in working with alcoholics, allowing him to feel confident and competent in dealing with a population which, though may be complicated, is ultimately largely rewarding. Requisite variety, then, is another description of the topic of this chapter. I would like to invite the reader to participate in a small exercise: Place your hands above your head and push your left hand against your right hand. Stop reading for a moment and notice your response. If you are like most people, your right hand will have pushed back against the left hand, leaving both hands above your head, in spite of the instruction. This virtually automatic response, learned however at some point in time, created one choice (pushing back with your right hand rather than pushing down with the left hand) and indicates how our internal repertoires automatically constrict, even if we have no particular investment in the result, such as in the above exercise. NLP's purpose then is for the client to have choice over the direction he desires his life to take. The way the alcoholic is "programmed" or has continued to program himself determines his interpretation of his experience and his resulting life choices.

Part of the presently existing treatment folklore contains the following smart rat metaphor. Researchers have two favorite populations they work with, rats and college students. In an experiment, a maze with seven tunnels is designed and cheese and its human equivalent are placed in the third tunnel. After some trial and error, both rat and human find the "cheese." The researchers then move the cheese to the seventh tunnel and after some time, the rat, not finding cheese in the third tunnel, will begin to experiment and will eventually find the cheese in the seventh tunnel. Here, then, lies the difference with humans, because human beings will continue to look for the cheese in the third tunnel, because it *ought* to be there. Congruently with this, no alcoholic ever gives up alcohol as a choice. Either the choice will be taken from him, or sufficient internal requisite variety needs to be built up so that, given that the organism naturally moves toward well-being, healthier choices than abusing alcohol almost automatically take the place of excessive drinking. Alcoholics use alcohol, as in the smart rat tale, not because it works, but because it "ought" to work—it did at some point in the past and the drinking behavior, though unproductive and frequently actually destructive, continues. Thus, since drinking originally did meet a need and therefore responded to a positive intent, the alcoholism counselor must keep in mind that drinking initially did constitute a successful strategy. The third tunnel did—at one time—contain the cheese. NLP then can provide the information and methodology necessary for the alcoholic to begin looking for where the cheese actually is in the present, and "install" strategies to enable this search. Thus, sorting mechanisms are what form the basis for successful execution of the basic programs for human behavior.

SORTING MECHANISMS

Each individual has a set of rules by which he makes sense out of his reality and his being part of this reality. NLP named these rules sorting mechanisms. The following sorting mechanisms are samples of the most prevalent damaged ones found in alcoholics and alcoholic systems. It is by no means a complete set of sorting mechanisms, since each individual has his own format for distinguishing his reality, internally and externally, and therefore his own requisite variety of these mechanisms. The sorting mechanisms described below indicate the ones shared by virtually all human beings, allowing for each individual's own additions and deletions, just like the commonality in all alcoholics is excessive drinking, allowing for each alcoholic's personal style in doing so. Each sorting mechanism described will be followed by examples out of the alcoholism treatment community.

In order to lead a satisfying life, each individual needs internal access to the following sorting mechanisms to bring order to a world that would otherwise appear chaotic. Access to sorting mechanisms allows for balanced choice making and coping skills. Thus, the fewer sorting mechanisms a client feels are available to him, the more constricted his area of functioning becomes. Therefore, the function of sorting strategies is to give direction to an unordered universe.

The first sorting mechanism relates to time usage.

1. In-Time versus Through Time. In-time connotes a state of being in the present without learning from the past or taking consequences of behavior into consideration. A "through-time" orientation is often synonymous with projection and a lack of being able to be in the present. Most alcoholics during their active drinking period as well as early sobriety, have exclusive access to the in-time mode. What this implies is (a) a total focus on the present, and (b) the absence of knowledge that "this too shall pass." What this means is that there is a need for immediate gratification without taking past learning or future consequences into consideration. Active alcoholics, upon starting their next binge, have virtual amnesia for the serious distress that followed the last binge. This appears not only to be, as was frequently thought, the defense mechanism called rationalization, but involves the particular orientation in time of alcoholics. Some alcoholics, however, function primarily in "through-time." These individuals extensively elaborate on the bad (or good but elusive) past and worry (or hope) for the future, but they are unable to enjoy or actually experience the present. Thus, the alcoholic who is only living in the present risks inattention to the consequences of his behavior, the client only living in the past is not likely to have sufficient motivation to get sober and those who live in the future do not effectively use past and present learning.

Since access to all three time modalities is essential in sobriety, it is important to carefully calibrate what the alcoholic has available to him.

In treating a dually-addicted young man it was discovered that since his father's suicide some three years prior to coming into treatment, he had been afraid of his own future, especially since a well-meaning counselor had told him that children of parents who commit suicide are a high suicide risk themselves. Not only was it important for this client to blank out the future, he had to make sure that there was no such thing and he managed to go through a substantial inheritance, allocated for his education, in a very short time, largely by buying LSD and designer drugs for his friends and himself. Conversely, a second male client, sober ten years, was worried about forgetting what the past had been like (he had spent twelve years in prison, partly as a result of a vehicular homicide committed while under the influence of alcohol). Though indigent when he was released from prison, he bought himself a pair of satin sheets in which he slept once or twice a week. This, he claimed, reminded him of the abysmal deprivation of prison he did not wish to return to, the availability of a good life in the present and motivation to make a good future. Jimmy had learned how to successfully make use of the two components of this sorting mechanism, in and through time. A young female client, abused as a child by her alcoholic father and abandoned by her prostitute mother, maintained a very flat, non-expressive posture in life. For her, also, there was no obvious merit in growing up, but being a child provided no safety either, so she decided on a kind of non-existence. When asked how she visualized her past, present, or future, she had surprisingly few memories (they appeared later in therapy), a non-participatory view of the present ("These things happen to me."), and a blank where an image of the future would be.

It is useful to develop a healthy combination of in-time and through-time mechanisms. For instance, it is important for an in-time part of a person to be playful, enjoy life, and for a through-time part of the individual to be logical, intellectual to choose actions leading to well-being.

A client recently presented me with a lovely metaphor of his life in regard to this time sort. In a session, the recovering alcoholic, sober one year, got in touch with a childpart inside and began a dialogue. At one point, he reported, his internal five-year-old asked him, in total amazement, "Are you the product of my misunderstanding?"

2. A second sorting mechanism involves a person's style of comprehension and planning, which NLP calls sorting by chunk size. Some people need to see and can only deal with the complete picture, whereas other people cope with life in an incremental way, one step at a time. Often in early sobriety, the recovering alcoholic will receive this advice, "One day at a time, easy does it, etc." Later on in sobriety, the counselor needs to calibrate the client's personal rhythm. Does he indeed make progress by taking small steps, or does he have to see a larger picture to remain motivated.

A female alcoholic, sober sixteen months, "working the program," was getting more and more depressed. Upon careful examination it appeared that by taking these small steps, the client was unable to define where her life was going. When she created a context for "one day at a time," mainly toward obtaining a much desired but so far unattainable college degree, her depression lifted and her "program" took on new meaning. In this case, the context of her life needed to be enlarged, she needed to "chunk up." In contrast, a young man in early recovery made plans to get his master's degree in business administration, but was unable to effectuate these plans until he enrolled in his first college course, completed it, and then was able to enroll in two courses at once. Another client was sober seven years and came into treatment because of severe depression, complaining that his life was not working. When asked what was not working, he stated, "Everything." Upon taking a closer look, it appeared that his working condition was excellent, his financial position enviable, his relationship with his children good, and his marriage dismal. This client had to "chunk down" before he could perceive the real cause of his depression and begin to deal with his difficulties in that particular area (adult intimate relationships).

3. The third prevalent sorting mechanism important in alcoholism treatment is sorting by being associated in an experience or dissociated. Imagine for a moment sitting on a park-bench watching

yourself in a rollercoaster. Then imagine yourself sitting in the rollercoaster, seeing the experience through your own eyes, feeling the experience. Some individuals will prefer sitting on the parkbench (dissociated), some being in the rollercoaster (associated). Of course, like all mechanisms, a healthy individual has access to both modalities. When a client is at a dance, she needs to be able to enjoy herself, but when she goes home to an actively alcoholic spouse, she needs to be able to dissociate, take distance, let it go. As a therapist it is important to check if a client can enjoy a feeling in a particular situation, or, on the flip side, gets totally enmeshed in a negative experience, or does the client have perspective, is able to take distance when appropriate, or, on the flip side again, is out of touch with his feelings. As before, the ideal situation for the client is access to each state, associated or dissociated, as it becomes appropriate in dealing with his life.

4. Moving Away from versus Moving Toward. This sorting mechanism is particularly important when assessing a client's motivation. Is the alcoholic motivated by moving away from a bad situation or by moving toward an attractive goal, a desired state. An alcoholic whose primary motivation is "moving away from" a particularly uncomfortable lifestyle is likely to lose this motivation once the pain is taken away or even diminished to a tolerable level. Examples of this mechanism are plentiful, but the most prevalent example is that of the abused wife, who, time and again moves back with her abusive spouse after a few days "because it really was not so bad" or "he did not mean it." Once an internal neutral zone is reached, the motivation gained from "moving away from" is lost, unless it can get connected to "moving toward," a movement toward a compelling future. Therefore, it is acceptable if the initial motivation is created by an uncomfortable life situation. However, to maintain this drive it needs to be coupled with an outcome as described in the chapter on rapport skills. An older female client, the child of two actively alcoholic parents, married a young, divorced man to escape the dreadful home situation. Pregnant some months later, she realized that her husband was an alcoholic who had been deserted by his first wife because of physical abuse. In her

hurry to move away from her past, Maria had not assessed what was available in her future that would validate her marriage as opposed to what had motivated her to leave home. Of course, it may just be as hazardous to only move toward a goal, since this does not allow for a level of satisfaction with achieved outcomes. People who have a "moving toward" orientation, are frequently the driven individuals, the workaholics, the perfectionists who cannot be satisfied at a given time, but only when goal X, and after that goal Y and Z, have been attained. As with the previously discussed sorting mechanisms, access to both modalities is the clue to achievement of a healthy lifestyle for the recovering alcoholic.

5. Internal versus External Reference. This sorting mechanism is closely related to how clients define reality. Does the alcoholic define the quality of his life by his internal standards or by the feedback he receives from others. Does he always check what others around him think and is he unable to decide on issues by himself, or does he "only listen to the sound of his own drummer" and does he have no mechanisms for incorporating external information.

An inner city policeman was so disliked by his colleagues that it was brought to the attention of his bureau's EAP. After extensive discussion in therapy it became clear that he "had gone inside" in early childhood being brought up by two alcoholic parents. Since he could—at that time—not trust information given to him by his parents, he developed a solid set of internal standards by which he lived. We found that not only did he have difficulties at work, but his wife was about to leave him and he had alienated three out of four of his children. This man needed to learn how to measure other people's reaction to him, something he, at a very young age, had trained himself never to do (see discussion on positive intent versus manifested behavior in the chapter on NLP as a conceptual base for alcoholism treatment). This client, who was basically a fine, sensitive, middle-aged man on the brink of full-blown alcoholism, needed to learn specific skills to measure other people's reactions to his actions, or even how to appropriately react to other people's actions. In this case it went as far as teaching him the value of smiling when smiled at, saying good morning when others said hello. The client was a good and dedicated student—all that was missing was his strategy for use of external reference. Conversely, therapists are quite familiar with the "pleaser," the person whose entire self-esteem rests on the feedback from others and who, therefore is almost continuously anxious, since it is impossible "to please all of the people all of the time." Often one sees a flip-flopping in the use of this mechanism in the process of getting sober. While drinking, the reference is frequently internal (what the alcoholic needs and wants). Then, in early sobriety, the recovering alcoholic may measure all of his feelings, thoughts, and actions against what he perceives the expectations are in his particular support systems such as AA. Eventually, when all goes well, a compromise between internal reference (deciding for oneself) and external reference (using information provided by important others, literature, etc.) may be reached.

6. The sixth sorting mechanisms will be demonstrated by the attitude of the counselor as well as the behavior of the client. This sorting mechanism is "downtime versus uptime." The difference in therapy is sympathy (crying for the client) versus empathy (joining the client in his model of the world or "walking a mile in his shoes" which is largely the equivalent of "uptime"). When working with a client it is essential to stay in "uptime," because that is how rapport is maintained (see chapter on NLP rapport skills and alcoholism treatment) and it is just as essential for the counselor, when he is not with a client, to be in "downtime," check his personal needs and attend to them, meditate, etc. An exception—as there are of course exceptions for all stated rules—is when the therapist on a rare occasion gets a feeling of danger when working with a client. It may be essential both for the safety of the therapist as well as the client to attend to this feeling, even at the cost of rapport. In terms of the alcoholic client, the uptime/downtime mechanism is an important skill as well. An alcoholic in an inpatient program had been silent in group for the first three weeks of treatment and no cajoling had made a difference in his attitude. He could inaccurately have been labeled resistant, but when the counselor began to obtain information regarding the process that took place in group for this alcoholic client, she found that the client became so preoccupied with his fears about large numbers of people that he actually was unable to notice what was really going on. Ingeniously she created a "group" of two people at which time the client was

able to stay in uptime. She then slowly increased the number of people who were part of the group, consistently paying attention to the client's sense of safety, until he was able to stay in "uptime" in the normal group setting. Naturally, only staying in "uptime" precludes accurate measuring of internal resources and again, the appropriate mix of uptime and downtime creates the most productive result for the client.

There are numerous other ways the therapist encounters the sorting mechanisms of alcoholics. A client can sort by activity, person, or location when he describes a new job to the therapist (the job is great because the work is real interesting, the job is terrible because the people are unfriendly, the job is nice because it is outdoors, etc.). A client can sort by "same or different" ("I want to do this because then I will be more like my friends," or "Because this will make me top man on the totem pole," etc.), by what is missing ("It was a nice party but there was no live music."), or by what is available ("We got there just in time to catch the second part of the show."), etc.

On a larger scale, then, the function of the sorting mechanisms is to determine for a significant part how the client executes the primary strategies that are identified as basic programs for human behavior. Thus, the sorting mechanisms assist in determining the skill level at which the client is functioning.

Robert Dilts, who has created some of the most important developments in the field of NLP over the past decade and is presently examining the possibilities of effecting changes in human belief systems and who has created a variety of strategies to accomplish this, has identified a number of these basic human programs. What follows is a description of these behavioral strategies in combination with short demonstrations from alcoholism treatment.

The basis strategies for human behavior are:

– Motivation
– Belief
– Creativity
– Memory
– Learning

– Reality
– Decision[1]

What specifically is a well-functioning strategy? Steve Drozdeck describes it as the process of TOTE:

> Test . . . Operate . . . Test . . . Exit, i.e., First Step: I am making this decision; Second Step: I am testing out my decision; Third Step: I am checking if my decision worked; Fourth Step: completion or moving on to the next item (congruence).[2] According to Dilts these strategies or programs are essential for achieving personal goals, graphically stated:[3]

The following is a summarized explanation and demonstration of the use of these human programs with the sorting mechanisms as a guide.

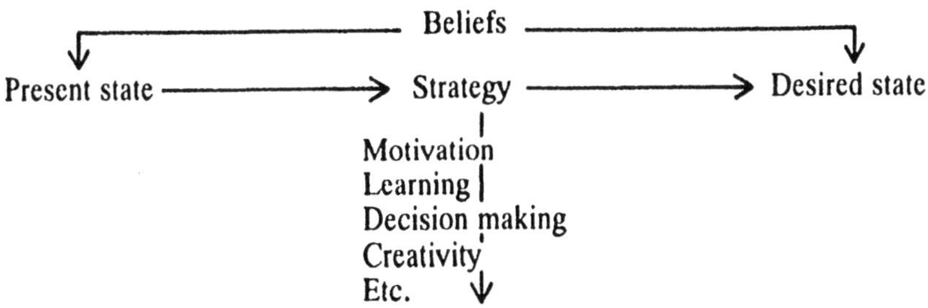

1. Motivation: In terms of the sorting mechanisms the pertinent questions the therapist may wish to ask herself when working with an alcoholic system is (a) does the client work in small segments or does he need to see the big picture (chunksize), (b) does he need to feel what it is like to achieve his goal (associated) or must he take a step back so that he does not drown in the effort (dissociated), (c) is he motivated by moving away from a bad situation or by the desired state he can move toward, and (d) does he measure success by what is expected from him or by what he himself feels is of value? To reiterate, generally, there is no advantage of one sorting skill over the other except in how it applies to the specific need in the given situation and the internal flexibility, the requisite variety of the client. For example, in working with a newly recovering alcoholic, the therapist found that the woman would have an anxiety attack

each time she began making plans for her future. The two essential changes that had to take place before she could actually focus on her next step in life was (a) to gain some perspective on her abilities and what was actually required of her (dissociate) and (b) to allow herself to "take things one step at a time" instead of focusing on the entire future (chunk down).

2. Belief: Naturally, it is essential for the therapist to be aware of how specifically the alcoholic shapes his belief, what in the past has allowed him to shift, i.e., from "I am incompetent" to "I am competent."

Dilts states that:

> Beliefs are generalizations about causation, meaning, and boundaries in the world around us, our capabilities and our identities. The most pervasive belief are those regarding our identity.[4]

Some examples of limiting beliefs about identity are: "I am helpless/worthless/a victim" (hopeless). Frequently, "the most difficult aspect of identifying a belief is that the ones that impact us the most are usually outside of our awareness."[5] For example: Jean, an active female alcoholic found that her beliefs about herself had been both determined by her mother ("You are unimportant.") and her father ("You are inferior."). As long as she held these beliefs about herself, she saw no reason to get sober. This frequently creates the loop that is popularly called "denial." Actually, Jean had no reason to get sober if she was unimportant and inferior, but she remained unimportant and inferior as long as she drank, which gave her no motivation to change. A belief change had to be effected simultaneously with obtaining sobriety in order to have Jean become willing to gain sobriety.

As a second demonstration, a young male client believed he was stupid, and each time he made a mistake, he reinforced this belief in himself by extensively reiterating the events in his life that showed him to be stupid. In treatment he learned to perceive mistakes as learning experience and eventually could proudly describe his mistakes in terms of what he learned from them.

A more humorous anecdote about the strength of beliefs is about the woman who pushed the button of the hot air hand drier in the ladies room, and, when the machine did not work, shrugged her shoulders and stated, "I guess they're out of hot air."

People are always guided by certain beliefs about the world and these beliefs themselves are guided by the previously discussed sorting mechanisms.

3. Creativity: A client's creativity involves developing new skills and strategies to cope with life situations. For instance, a female alcoholic, "discovered" that she could be assertive when she was verbally abused by her mother, rather than "drink at it." In order to explore your alcoholic client's creativity, it is important to examine his orientation in time, toward being associated or dissociated, the chunksize of his endeavors, the internal and external reference points and the uptime/downtime skills.

4. Memory: The question the therapist wants an answer to is what does the client retain from his experiences that he can use toward his future well being. Some of the sorting mechanisms that the recovering alcoholic needs to have access to are (a) the in-time versus through-time mechanism. A "double trouble" client, a mentally ill chemical abuser had two related thought processes that had made his behavior in therapy cyclic for years. In the first place, he did not know how to distinguish between memory and present reality. Thus, the short homosexual episode coupled with overwhelming guilt kept appearing as an event in the present, preventing any current heterosexual relationship. Secondly, memory being selective, he remembered the bad parts of the past events, but had no memory for how he had terminated the homosexual relationship and had moved into a what he considered for himself a more appropriate heterosexual relationship. The memory strategy of an individual then determines where past events are on the persons "timeline" and what is internally selected to become a memory and therefore a significant part of a person's identity. It is many an alcoholism counselor's experience that an alcoholic, frequently prior to a slip, can have virtual amnesia for his own previous drinking history and their consequences ("My drinking was not so bad, it was my wife who caused the trouble.") and in contrast, the alcoholic in early recovery may state in a bout of depression, "I have wasted my whole life."

A second important sorting mechanism in the memory strategy is "moving away from versus moving toward." When "designing" a memory strategy for an alcoholic client, it is essential to connect it to the future, so that no internal loop is created, which might keep the client tied to the past.

A client needs a memory strategy for a number of reasons, the most important one being the need for each individual to have an identity which includes the memory of past events and of himself within these events. The second important element of the memory strategy is the client's ability to use past experiences to learn from. Another significant part of the memory strategy is to sort events in accordance with these events truly being in the past. Too frequently, a past event will present itself over and over again in the present, in a loop-like fashion. Recently, I worked with a seventy-two year old alcoholic who blamed his drinking on the birth of his sister who became the family's favorite when he was six. Thus, congruently with this, an important element of the memory strategy is finding the associated/dissociated sorting skill of the alcoholic client. "Having perspective" is an essential part of a well-functioning memory strategy.

5. Learning Strategy: Of course, no one can survive independently without reliance on skill in learning life's essential requirements and in fact, AA as well as most in-patient programs and all outpatient care greatly depend on the alcoholic's innate ability for learning, and learning quickly. Enormous amounts of knowledge about how to live a sober life and the dangers of giving up sobriety are disseminated in alcoholism treatment programs ("lectures") and AA meetings (the "metaphors," or the stories at speaker meetings) often in a direct teaching way but frequently also more indirectly through modeling and sharing, allowing the alcoholic his own interpretations and style for integrating the new learning into his own life. Significant sorting strategies are of course chunk size and internal versus external reference.

6. Reality Strategy: Counselors sometimes may have the feeling that what the client experienced during an incident in a treatment program is quite different from the counselor's perception of reality. For example, a middle-aged male client had disrupted many group sessions and lectures by being late, and once he was there,

being loud and inappropriate. The primary counselor and another counselor decided to have a quiet discussion with him to see if they could turn the behavior around. The conversation went very well. The two counselors happily reported in staff that afternoon that the client was adjusting well. The counselors were therefore shocked to discover upon leaving the meeting that the man had checked out AMA saying, "I knew they were out to get me." One of the most significant mechanisms therefore in a well-functioning reality strategy is "internal reference versus external reference," the ability of the client to accurately assess external information and translate it appropriately as an internalized experience. The above mentioned client had suffered much rejection in his life and had no available mechanism for fitting the care and concern of the counselors into his internal model of the world.

7. Decision Making: This skill is of particular significance in alcoholism recovery. How and when does the alcoholic actually decide to get sober, remain sober, leave a painful relationship, get a better job. What internal model does he need to have available to make appropriate life choice. A young male client had a particular decision loop that occurred several times a year. He would stop drinking and begin building himself up. An incident would happen and this client would decide that he would always be the victim at which point he would have a slip. The way out of a slip involved another decision, namely that no matter how "the world" dumped on him, he had to keep moving upwards at which point the young man would sober up again. Sorting mechanisms examined in this context were his ability to calibrate in uptime versus downtime, his moving away from versus moving toward, and an internal versus external reference in addition to his own mechanism of sorting for negative external events as motivation for decision making.

SUMMARY AND CONCLUSION

The recovering alcoholic's success in maintaining sobriety is at least for a significant part due to having a full range of well-functioning basic human programs available to him. Each basic human program is supported by a set of sorting mechanisms that bring order into the information the client receives internally and externally. Rather than defining particular behavior as denial or resistance, it is useful for the therapist to first determine the client's thought patterns and behaviors in terms of what he has internally available in the realm of effective human programs and sorting mechanisms, since these skills largely determine how he copes, and in the future will cope, with life events.

REFERENCES

1. Dilts, R., Conference Literature, ENLPI, unpublished, 1985.
2. Drozdeck, S., Conference Literature, ENLPI, unpublished, 1984.
3. Dilts, R., Conference Literature, ENLPI, unpublished, 1985.
4. Ibid.
5. Ibid.

Chapter 9

Neuro-Linguistics as a Treatment Modality for Alcoholism and Substance Abuse

Matthew J. Tierney

The Law of Third's states that one-third of your client population will get better regardless of how good or bad you, as a counselor, may be. One-third will get better because of their strong motivation to get better coupled with the assistance, skills, and knowledge that the counselor has to offer. The last third is the one-third that will get better only if the counselor has the ability to create change in the client's perspective of the world, despite limited motivation and little conscious belief, on the client's part, of his or her ability to get better. It is this last one-third that requires us as alcoholism/substance abuse counselors to develop highly diversified skills if we are to increase our success rate.

I first want to salute all of the anonymous groups that have done an effective job in helping many people recover from alcoholism and other substance abuses, whatever the drug involved. Groups such as Alcoholics Anonymous (AA), Narcotics Anonymous (NA), and Pills Anonymous (PA), supply many sought after, necessary, and valuable resources. Comradery, support, information, structure, and guidance are some of the invaluable resources available through these organizations and traditional treatment approaches to alcoholism/substance abuse. One-third of the client population will respond positively to these approaches because they are in that group that are going to get better regardless. The second-third will respond positively to the AA model because the particular resources as they are presented in that model meet the individual's specific needs. My concern is with the individuals that do not respond favorably to the traditional treatment models.

Over the years, I have, in private practice, successfully treated many individuals from this latter group. They have made certain comments to me over and over again. "If I wanted to be with a bunch of drunks I'd stay at a bar." "If I wanted to hear 'don't drink' I'd stay home." I'd rather be drunk than in therapy for the rest of my life." "I don't want their kind of religion." In sorting through such comments, I became aware of prevalent issues and needs of these clients that the traditional approaches to alcoholism/substance abuse were not addressing.

One of the issues which require us as alcoholism/substance abuse counselors to expand our skills is this group's views on dependency issues. AA applies the concept that being with other recovering alcoholics is supportive. However, the clients of whom I speak perceive being with other recovering individuals as "being thrown in with a bunch of ex-drunks who have a 'better than thou' attitude." These clients laugh at the slogan "Don't drink and go to meetings," saying that if not drinking were that easy there would be no need for meetings. Bringing themselves into a group for treatment is too difficult a first step for them. They require a different kind of support.

A second important issue for this traditionally unresponsive group is that they perceive the directive to attend meetings forever as a lifelong punishment or sentence. What the directive implies is a built-in helplessness. It is making the statement that they will never really be okay. For these clients the translation is, "If I'm never going to be better, I don't have a reason to make an effort." The suggestion that they will always need help and not be okay generates a fear of giving up the only coping mechanism (drinking) that at least has offered them temporary relief from not being okay.

A third issue which limits traditional approaches for this special needs group is that to date the focus of treatment has been to change behavior through negative directives. "Don't drink, don't hang out with those that do, don't go where they are, don't do what you used to do." Even the infamous "You should" statements imply that one is doing something that one shouldn't be doing. I remember a client telling me that he didn't return to AA because at his first meeting he was told that he should have gone to the meeting in White Plains, not the meeting that he did show up for in Scarsdale. He left feeling lost and that he had once again failed and done something wrong.

Negative directives diminish self-esteem in any population. When you are dealing with a population whose self-esteem is already precariously low, negative directives are emotionally devastating. Secondly, this is a group who come with a long history of having been directed in what not to do. It has been my experience that many of this group have developed an automatic oppositional response to negative directives. Further, such directives leave the person with a void of knowledge, telling you what not to do without providing information on what to do. What they need is to be given information to fill the void.

In traditional treatment techniques the focus has been on symptom removal. The assumption is that recovering substance abusers are going to be okay as long as they don't drink and go to meetings. The effort has been to change overt behaviors while paying little attention to the underlying dynamic structure producing the behaviors. It is my experience that for many individuals the process must be reversed. Lasting behavior change comes, for many, only after the emotional and dynamic underpinnings of the behavior have been attended to.

Traditionally the approach has been detoxification, abstinence, attend meetings, and then deal with unresolved emotional issues. In my mind, this is asking the client to walk around with a time bomb strapped to his or her chest with no notion of when it might go off. Many individuals need to deal with the emotional issues earlier in treatment for change to occur.

Lastly, traditional treatment approaches are limited by their own scripts. More specifically, it is the generalization of the same script to all who come for help which becomes limiting. I believe that we do an injustice to our clients when we get caught in a belief loop which states that, since something worked in the past, it should work in the same way for all others in the future. Traditional approaches assume that their's is a safe and sound approach for all clients. It is not.

I believe that, for those people for whom AA approaches have been ineffective, much of the cause is related to the fact that the script did not meet the unique emotional and situational needs of the individual. The traditional script does not start at a point which makes it possible for those individuals from the challenging unresponsive last one-third to feel safe enough to risk change. Rather, the AA script begins several chapters ahead of them. To assist this final third to recovery, we, as counselors, must go beyond the self-imposed limitations of traditional treatment techniques for alcoholism and other substance abuses.

Neuro-Linguistic Programming (NLP) encompasses both a philosophical base and therapeutic techniques which I have found extremely useful in my work with alcoholic/substance abuse clients. To begin, NLP emphasizes the positive. NLP stresses being positive in both attitude and presentation. This positive approach includes talking in positives, giving directives in positives, and seeking positives in all behaviors. A basic NLP belief is that there is some positive intent or purpose to all behavior. I seek out that positive intent in all my clients' behaviors, even their most destructive behaviors. I find out very specifically what it is they are trying to accomplish by their drinking and/or abuse of other substances. Then I guide them to find other ways to accomplish that goal.

As opposed to one script for all, the NLP position is that to assist people, we, as counselors, must be flexible and meet individuals in their model of the world. An individual's model of the world consists of that person's beliefs, values, perceptions, ways of organizing and representing thoughts, and internal resources.

All too often counselors want clients to enter the counselor's model of the world. If the alcoholic could do that, he or she wouldn't be a client. We must be willing to accept, as opposed to fight and confront, an individual's beliefs, internal organizing processes, and resources, I utilize my clients' beliefs and perceptions as opposed to trying to wear the client down and then impose new beliefs on them, or worse, impose my beliefs and resources on them.

Working from the client's organization of the world is important for several reasons. The first is that it facilitates communication. We, as human beings, process and organize information through our senses. Whether through internal dialogue (talking to ourselves) or mind's eye pictures (visual images), our thought processes have a sensory base. When a client uses pictures to represent a thought or belief, I match that internal representation by using visual language (How do you see that?, What is your view about?) in talking with the client about that belief. Matching our language to the way in which an individual represents information, allows the input to be more readily understood and accepted.

A second reason for meeting a client in their model of the world is that by having the client recognize and utilize their own perceptions, beliefs, and resources, the client progresses at a pace and in a way that ensures that the changes are ecologically safe. Changes must fit a person's ecology, i.e., the person's individual and personal environment as it exists, in order for changes to be lasting. The client needs to be able to live comfortably with the changes.

A third reason for meeting clients in their model of the world is that working from this model insures that the recognition for creating appropriate and constructive changes goes to the client. Getting recognition for creating change builds self-esteem and makes it easier for the client to create more changes.

As alcoholism/substance abuse counselors, we have the opportunity to work with an extremely creative and imaginative client population. Prior to the last stages of the alcoholic progression, the alcoholic/substance abuser is manipulative, devious, cunning, and conniving. Traditional treatment views these qualities as part of the client's sickness. Rather than condemning these qualities, the NLP approach is to tap and utilize the resources, the imagination and creativity, that made it possible for the individual to be manipulative, devious, cunning, and conniving. It is not the resources, but the direction of the resources, which must be altered. Clients must be assisted to identify, acknowledge and redirect the specific resources available to them.

To redirect resources, I first link the person's resources, such as creativity and imagination, to the tools of survival which the client has developed, such as manipulation and deviousness. I show the client how it requires a great deal of imagination and creativity to juggle family, job, and alcohol as he or she has done. Once the client accepts these resources as their own, I assist him or her to now use the resources differently.

Our client population is famous for now accepting responsibility for their lives and/or the condition of their lives. They assign blame for everything wrong in their lives to something or someone outside of themselves. They refer to their addiction or alcoholism as something that "happened" to them as opposed to something that is happening. It is my experience that as long as a person can keep him or herself in reaction to the past they can avoid responsibility for the present. If a person is in reaction, they cannot take constructive action. NLP stresses the importance of the development of individual responsibility.

One way I start the process toward individual responsibility is with a series of questions. The majority of clients have a ready list of answers to "why" questions such as "Why are you here?", they are comfortable answering "why" questions. I ask "what" questions, "What is your reason for being here?", "What is your reason for drinking?", "What is your reason for continuing a destructive behavior?" What questions keep the client more focused on the present and less in reaction to the past.

When I get a litany of reasons for drinking, I say, "Those were the reasons for starting, now what are the reasons for continuing?" I began in their model of the world by giving recognition to their reasons for drinking. I then move them forward and give them responsibility for continuing or changing.

NLP looks beyond symptom removal. NLP techniques are designed to change behavior (remove symptoms) by changing the individual's internal perceptual structure both conscious and subconsciously. A goal of treatment is to modify the beliefs and perceptions which limit the client. Such modifications open up new choices and possibilities which enable the client to then change behaviors.

Throughout treatment I ask a lot of questions in very particular ways to create perceptual changes. One very effective questioning technique is to preface certain questions with the statement, "Answer this question silently." The alcoholic/substance abuser has learned well to lie to others and meet challenges through lies to others. Having the individual answerable only to him or herself creates an internal loop in which the individual is held accountable for their answer. Their usual escape route is gone.

Another questioning technique I use to ask clients to let their imaginations run wild with the question, "If you make such and such a change, what is the worst that could happen?" "If you make this change, what is the best that could happen?" Such questions open up options and possibilities as well as allow clients to ponder consequences.

I find it extremely effective to change the internal perspective of the alcoholism/addiction, or, in NLP terms, reframe the addiction. I often reframe the alcoholism/addiction as a "spent solution" to a problem. After the reframe, the goal is to overcome the old, inadequate solution. To accomplish this, I first find out how the client overcame obstacles to becoming an alcoholic. As I stated earlier, it requires a great deal of creativity to become a successful drunk. Then I take the tools and resources the person used to overcome obstacles to becoming addicted and begin to apply these tools to new options. I assist the client to tie his or her resources to new solutions and away from the alcoholism/addiction or old solution. The client then begins to generate options and choices toward recovery.

Many of the clients I encounter honestly do not believe they can get better. They are limited by their own beliefs about themselves. Actually, they are limited by someone else's beliefs that they have accepted.

For example, Katherine R. is a successful woman, housewife, mother, and teacher. She is the adult child of alcoholic parents. Her drinking pattern began secretly and continued to the point of being covert-overt. Katherine is one of four children and has four children of her own. She was the mirror of her mother, including her mother's drinking.

We covered some initial ground work and in response to "What is your reason for drinking?" Katherine answered, "This sounds stupid, but it's all I know." Further questioning revealed that Katherine's belief was that she was going to end up exactly like her mother—dead drunk. My next statement to her was one of agreement. I told her I believed that she believed that to be true. I said that what I needed to know now was how she knew that she believed this. Katherine didn't know how she knew and felt stupid and inadequate because she couldn't answer the question. Most clients respond similarly.

I reassured Katherine that most people can't answer that question the first time they hear it. I then asked her to ponder the last time she heard that belief. By watching and listening to her, I had learned that Katherine had a very strong internal dialogue going on. Asking the question in her model of how she represented this belief (auditorily), made it easy for her to answer the question. "Five minutes ago," she said. I now again asked her how she knew the belief. It was because she could hear herself saying it. I then asked her to recall the first time that she heard the belief. Katherine was twelve when she first heard the statement that she was just like her mother. Slowly and calmly I asked her to remember the belief and to now recognize whose voice it was when she heard it. The voice was her mother's. My next question was "Whose belief was it, your's or your mother's?" "It was mom's," was the reply.

It is at this point that all too often an error is made. Counselors will frequently confront beliefs. Beliefs are the core of our identity and when challenged or confronted put us in a defensive mode. A confrontation at this point would have brought forward Katherine's defenses, challenged the mother-daughter relationship, and generated intense anger. What I went on to do was to create doubt in the original belief which made room to create alternate beliefs.

To create doubt, I asked questions. Keeping my tones soft and my tempo even, I asked Katherine, "Was your mother ever wrong about anything?"

"I guess so. Yes," was the answer.

"Was your mother like your grandmother?"

"No, granny was warm."

"Is it remotely possible that your mother ever said anything in error?"

"Yeah."

> "Is it at all possible that she had a positive intent?"
>
> "I don't know what you mean."
>
> "Could she, just maybe, have been trying to scare you, to motivate you?"
>
> "I doubt it."
>
> "Did your mother have any inadequacies?"
>
> "Oh, yeah."
>
> "Begin answering these next questions silently, only for yourself. When you think about that time now, is it just remotely possible your mother was in error? Is it remotely possible that her statement was born of her inadequacies? It is possible for you to imagine what your grandmother would have said in that same situation?"

Another piece of work that was very successful with Katherine is one that I often use to get clients out of reaction and active in their own life and recovery. I call this intervention "The Garden Peace."

I asked Katherine to sit back, close her eyes and imagine the garden I was about to describe. I asked her to listen to my words and in her mind paint whatever pictures she sees as I speak.

> Imagine a field with a small stream running through it. A bridge spans the stream and you are standing in the middle of the bridge. Imagine looking to your left and seeing this portion of the garden. It is grass and trees, shrubs and thorns. It is in disarray. It is obvious this part of the garden has not been tended to. If you use a little bit more imagination you might even hear the stream running through the garden. We will call this portion of the garden your past. History. Turning to your right is the open portion of the garden. You now have the opportunity to plant what you choose in what is your future garden. Ponder what has been and as you stand on the bridge in the present ponder the future. You, Katherine, can now plant or build your life and garden. You can bring whatever you choose from the past or leave it there. It is your garden, your life. You tend it.

"The Garden Peace" is a powerful metaphor for several reasons. It utilizes the client's desires, allows the client to face their past from a safe distance, and offers the opportunity for the client to create their own change. Drinking became one of the rocks Katherine left in the past portion of her garden.

In this next case study I present a version of what I call "The Journey Peace." "The Journey Peace" is both a learning experience and a rescue mission.

John S. is 43 years old, a truck driver, a widower, and the father of three girls. He is funny, intelligent, loving, and protective. John, as so many clients, was a dual abuser, a drinker, and cocaine user. He had been brought up in a physically and emotionally abusive household. His father was the emotional abuser and his mother the physical abuser.

John originally came to me with the question, "How do I beat the drugs?" John clarified what he wanted. He wanted to be stronger than the drugs. He wanted to still take them, but be in control.

I asked John, "If he had ever gotten high?"

"Yes," was John's answer.

"Drunk?"

"Yes."

"Sick?"

"Yes."

"Passed out?"

"Yes."

"Blacked out?"

"Yes."

"Loss of memory?"

"Yes."

"In trouble from drinking?"

Two DWI's and three arrests for fighting qualified as a yes.

"Snorted coke?"

"Yes."

"Gotten the rush?"

"Yes."

"Partied hard with the coke set?"

"Yes."

"Gotten anxious?"

"Yes."

"Gotten paranoid?"

"Yes."

"What else do you want from the drugs? They have nothing else to offer you but death. You've already beaten them. You've gotten everything alcohol and cocaine have to offer. Stopping now means you're stronger than the drugs. YOU WIN!"

That he had already gotten everything the drugs (alcohol and cocaine) had to offer represented an entirely new perspective for John. He had never before defined "stronger than" as stopping.

Several sessions later I began setting the ground work with John for "The Journey Peace." I wanted him to be able to look at experiences in his life with a mind-set that allowed for error. To get this mind-set, I drew on the feelings and attitudes John had, when years earlier, he watched his children learn to walk. We talked about his children and how they took their first steps and how proud he was of them. I held him at that moment of pride. I told him to close his eyes and picture those precious moments of each child's first step. He did and was smiling as a tear fell out of the corner of one eye.

As he continued to reflect I told him that he was now ready to go on a journey. I told him that the only luggage he would need for this journey was the understanding and freedom from judgment that he had for his children when they were learning to walk. It was this understanding that made his children's first steps and the falls that followed successes rather than failures.

I asked John to imagine a movie house, any movie house, and to imagine he was walking toward and through the doors to the movie screen area.

> It is getting darker and you are to choose a seat in the middle of the theater and be seated. Remember a time when you were twenty and a time when you were twelve. Chose okay times, nothing great or terrible, just okay. Now imagine the twelve-year-old sitting in the front row and the twenty-year-old sitting midway between you and the child. The screen is blank and the theater is quiet. Become aware of the caretaker part of you. You know the one. It is the part of you that cares for your daughters and has kept you alive. Now become aware of the survivor part of you, you know, your warrior part. Imagine the caretaker sitting in the seat at your left, close to your heart, and the warrior sitting next to your strong right arm. The journey will now begin. Allow your mind's eye to project on the screen your earliest childhood memories. This is your movie and it is for you to learn from. Watch as your memories become a motion picture and you learn what you need to learn from them. Some memories might be deemed pleasant and they can now become just learning experiences. As you continue bringing this movie forward in time, learn all you need to learn.

At this point John said that the kid was scared and getting hurt.

> "For what, by whom, where?" I asked, instructing him to answer silently. "Was the kid doing something terrible or just being a kid doing kid things?"
>
> "Just being a kid," he answered.
>
> "John, in your mind's eye have the twenty-year-old-you go down to the twelve-year-old-you and tell him he is going to be okay. Use these words, 'I am you of the future and we are going to be okay.' Now, in your mind's eye have them both walk back to the twenty-year-old's seat and continue the journey."

John was not comfortable proceeding.

At the point in the movie when John was twenty-five he began to cry. This was the time in his life when his wife died. She was killed in an auto accident and died of internal injuries. When I asked John what was going on inside for him, his reply was "If only I were driving, she would be alive today."

I had John bring the twelve and twenty-year-olds to sit with the present-day him and for a moment and mourn their loss. Then I had him describe his picture of the accident scene. He had himself included in the picture of the accident. In reality he had not been at the accident scene. His feelings of guilt for not being able to change what had happened to his wife put him in the picture. He didn't belong in the picture of the accident. I asked John what he could have done back then to make things different. What he answered was that he couldn't have done anything because he had to be home with the girls. We corrected the pictures and John was able to let go of the self-imposed guilt.

John's movie continued. At the completion, I had him refocus on the drinking and drug use. I asked John if he could understand how at first the drinking and later the cocaine use actually served a purpose.

"Yeah, it got me through a lot," he said.

"John, can you now see how neither is still serving a purpose, but that you, John, are now serving the drugs."

"They're ugly," he said.

"John, do you desire to stop them now or later?"

"Now."

"John, create five alternate behaviors for yourself that are appropriate, constructive, and okay for you to use in any situation that might generate a desire to escape."

"I don't understand."

"John, who survived your childhood?"

"Me."

"What made that possible?"

"I talked to myself and read and imagined. Hey, that's what I did in my movie. I saved me."

"Right-on John."

John learned from his past experiences that he could survive, that he had options, that he had resources. In John's words, "I have a sense of freedom. I really can do things."

It was not within the scope of this article to provide detailed descriptions of NLP techniques. What I hoped to do, through discussion and case studies, was to stimulate your curiosity and introduce some new choices for you in your own work.

Both Katherine and John were seen several times before and after the interventions described in this article were used. These techniques are tools. Before any change technique can be successful, a trusting relationship must be formed between client and counselor. My clients come to trust me because I put their behavior aside and search for the person. Judgment about behavior is suspended. I never try to take any options away. My purpose is to add appropriate, constructive choices by expanding on the client's resources. When my work is done, the old behaviors are gone, the person remains to go forward. Our clients give us the information we need to help them. It is our creativity in applying what they give us that is the deciding factor in creating change. There is no such thing as a resistant client, only a client with a lack of flexibility.

The most important thing that I did for Katherine and John was to help them create a model of the world for themselves that was flexible, contained choices, and was a good fit for them as individuals. With such a model they were able to assume responsibility for creating change. Isn't that what it's all about?

Chapter 10

A Neuro-Linguistic Programming Perspective on Codependency

Ann M. Gardner, PhD

INTRODUCTION

Case Example A

B.J., a successful independent businesswoman in her early forties came for help with "stress management." She indicated that she had really wanted her husband to come for help, because "if he would just quit drinking there wouldn't be so much stress in my life." She reported that since he was frequently out of work, she had to assume primary responsibility for supporting the family, which included two daughters, age 6 and 8. She admitted that she was a perfectionist where her children and home were concerned, but that she "just can't get through to T.J. (her husband)."

Case Example B

K.T. is a young professional woman in her late twenties who entered therapy to make career decisions and to address issues related to the dissolution of her 9 year marriage. She had recently divorced her husband; the divorce had been precipitated by an assault and threat to her life by him. She reported that he had beaten her on several other occasions, and that he had been drinking heavily prior to each of these incidents. When asked if her ex-husband had a drinking problem, she replied, "He didn't drink all that often, but when he did, he drank too much and always got mean." She also reported that she had been physically abused as a young child both by her mother and by her father who "definitely had a drinking problem."

Case Example C

K.F. is a free-lance graphic artist in his early thirties who has had twelve months of sobriety in AA. During his initial therapy session, however, he reported that he has not been able to "get his life started again." He described himself as having "no motivation" and feeling like "nothing is worth doing." When asked about his childhood, he said "Not exactly great. I know now that my dad is an alcoholic—and anytime anything went wrong, I was the one who got it." Verbal and physical abuse and extreme punishments like being tied up inside a closet characterized his life before leaving home to go to college.

In spite of their diversity of life experience and presenting problems, these three clients have one characteristic in common—each is, or has been, involved in a significant relationship with an alcoholic. Each can be characterized as "codependent." Both clients B and C are adult children of alcoholics (ACOAs); both clients A and B have been involved in codependent relationships as adults.

DEFINITION OF CODEPENDENCY

The term "codependency" has been used in the chemical dependency field to refer to the disruptive behavior patterns and personal belief systems which emerge when an individual's life "becomes unmanageable as a result of living in a committed relationship with an alcoholic" (Gorski and Miller, 1984) or other chemically dependent person. While this chapter emphasizes codependent relationships with alcoholics, recently the concept of codependency has been extended to adult children of alcoholics, victims of child or spouse abuse, and people in relationships with emotionally or mentally disturbed individuals.

Beattie (1987) defines the codependent person as "one who has let another person's behavior affect him or her, and who is obsessed with controlling that person's behavior." Subby (1984) defines codependency as "An emotional, psychological, and behavioral condition that develops as a result of an individual's prolonged exposure to, and practice of, a set of oppressive rules—rules which prevent the open expression of feeling as well as the direct discussion of personal and interpersonal problems."

CHARACTERISTICS OF THE CODEPENDENT PERSON

Another paper in this monograph describes the effects of alcoholism on the alcoholic's entire family. Black (1981) has reported common patterns that emerge among children of alcoholics (COAs): the "responsible child" who assumes a caregiver role in the family; the "acting out" or "scapegoat" child whose frequent misbehavior takes the focus of attention away from the alcoholic; the "adjuster," who appears to be unaffected by the problem but who may no longer feel in control of his/her own life; and the "placater" who assumes responsibility for resolving conflicts in the family. Wegscheider-Cruse (1981) uses somewhat different terms, but also emphasizes the consistent emergence of these roles and the high probability that COAs will carry these roles into their adult lives. The codependent spouse, who has a high probability of also being an ACOA (Subby and Friel, 1984) assumes parallel roles in the family system (Beattie, 1987).

Throughout the literature there is a consistent recognition of common issues faced by many codependent individuals, and an emphasis on helping codependent individuals recognize the importance of addressing their own recovery rather than continuing to focus attention on the alcoholic's problems (Beattie, 1987).

Neuro-Linguistic Programming (NLP) provides a useful framework for understanding these patterns and offers several effective tools for intervening to break the cycle of codependency. This chapter addresses three major issues: (1) control; (2) definition of self; and (3) trust and intimacy. These codependency issues are discussed within the context of belief systems and metaprograms, the patterns or filters each individual uses in operating in the world and processing information.

BELIEF SYSTEMS

Robert Dilts, one of the major developers within the field of NLP, has done extensive work on belief systems. His work provides insight into understanding how codependency patterns are formed. Beliefs are the guiding principles that provide direction to an individual's behavior. Dilts explains how beliefs serve as "generalizations about causation, meaning, and boundaries in the world around us, our capabilities, and our identity" (Dilts, Hallbom, and Smith, in press, 1990). Frequently, codependent individuals have a cluster of limiting beliefs that lead to interference in attaining goals in many areas of their lives. Codependent individuals may manifest this interference in different ways. For example, both Clients A and B described at the beginning of the chapter have successful careers; yet, all three have experienced difficulties in their personal relationships.

Dilts et al. (1990) identify several ways limiting beliefs can interfere in an individual's life. They term these the "Seven Cs":

- *Confusion*: A lack of clarity about goals and steps for achieving goals;

  The inconsistency that children of alcoholics experience as they are growing up or the day-to-day inconsistencies that are so characteristic of life with an alcoholic often result in confusion. The pattern of denial so pervasive in alcoholic families compounds the problem.

- *Content*: Misinformation and improper raw materials;

  Again, the pervasive pattern of denial of feelings and actual facts contributes to interference.

- *Catastrophes*: Past traumas and negative imprints from personal history;

Many COAs are abused by alcoholic parents, either verbally or physically. Child neglect, a more subtle yet equally damaging form of maltreatment, is also common. Spouse abuse is also frequently present in alcoholic families. With or without such a history of traumatic experiences, however, the codependent individual lives through numerous negative interactions. Dilts (1987) defines an imprint as "a significant experience from the past in which a person formed a belief or cluster of beliefs." When these imprint experiences are negative, the effects on the individual's beliefs about themselves can be detrimental.

- *Comparison*: inappropriate expectations and criteria;

  COAs are frequently subjected to expectations that are neither age-appropriate nor realistic. A reversal of the parent/child role is quite common. Similarly, spouses of alcoholics often have inappropriate expectations that the alcoholic will change and/or unrealistic expectations of his/her own ability to stay in control and to cope with the situation.

- *Conflict*: Incongruency, secondary gain, and hidden agendas;

  All of these patterns are extremely common in alcoholic homes.

- *Context*: External impediments;

  Alcoholic families are often faced with limited resources, both in terms of their life circumstances and in terms of the flexibility to deal with the situation.

- *Conviction*: Doubt about achieving goals;

  Many codependent individuals experience serious doubts about their own self-worth and abilities.

Dilts (1987) points out that these interferences can lead to an impasse in an individual's life. For the codependent person, this impasse is likely to manifest itself on the identity level as low self-esteem and a sense of:

- *Helplessness*:

  The individual's belief that goals are possible but that she/he is not capable of achieving them;

- *Hopelessness*:

  The individual's belief that goals are not achievable regardless of his/her capabilities; or

- *Worthlessness*:

  The individual's belief that she/he does not deserve specific goals because of something she/he is or has or has not done.

METAPROGRAMS

The human brain processes information by organizing it into categories. Leslie Cameron-Bandler, one of the early developers in NLP, identified Metaprograms, the internal comparison filters by which the brain accomplishes this organization. They provide the structure that governs what information the brain attends to, how the information is interpreted, and the direction of subsequent behavior. The metaprograms an individual utilizes will vary according to the situation, and are, to a large extent, determined by the individual's past history. In addition, each metaprogram represents a continuum. It is also important to point out that there is no "correct" pattern within each continuum; however, extremes at either end can reflect limited behavioral choices.

Bailey (1986) developed the first comprehensive tool for assessing Metaprograms. James and Woodsmall (1988) delineate a total of twenty metaprograms. Eight of these patterns are particularly useful for understanding the major issues of codependency. The correlations with codependency patterns described below are merely suggestive, based on an analysis of verbal patterns of twenty-two clients with a history of codependency. More systematic research on the correlations between these metaprograms and codependency patterns is warranted; nonetheless, the following preliminary descriptions provide a useful foundation for intervening with codependent clients.

- *Toward/Away From*:

This continuum indicates whether a person is motivated primarily to move toward positive goals and what she/he wants or to avoid or move away from what she/he does not like or want. Given the high degree of stress in the lives of codependent individuals, it is understandable why they are more likely to be motivated to move away from than toward.

- *Possibility/Obligation*:

This is the other critical motivational filter. It indicates whether the individual does things primarily because they want or choose to or because they feel they have to or must do them. Individuals who are bound by obligation or necessity operate under the constraints of many rules and are apt to believe there is only one right way to do things. As previously mentioned, Subby (1984) considers the constraints of oppressive rules to be the fundamental basis of codependency. Members of alcoholic families have often learned to operate out of such tight constraints as a mode of survival and self-protection (Gravitz and Bowden, 1985).

- *Internal/External Frame of Reference*:

This metaprogram determines how people judge the results of their actions; whether they use their own internal criteria as the foundation for their judgements or whether they are dependent on outside sources for approval or judgment. Too often, the codependent individual has come to doubt his or her own judgment and relies too heavily on outside approval or an external source of validation.

- *Primary Interest*:

This filter indicates whether an individual is interested primarily in people, places, things, activities, or information. Codependents will vary across this spectrum, but it is possible that the primary interest sort will correlate with their role in the family: Responsible/Caregiver-Information and/or People;

Adjuster-Things; Scapegoat-Activities or Places; Placator-People.

- *Match/Mismatch*:

  This filter indicates what a person attends to in order to understand something: does he or she attend primarily to similarities or to differences, or do they attend to both? Again the codependent's patterns may be related to the role she/he plays in the family system. Among the twenty-two clients interviewed, there was a preponderance of mismatch responses which may be reflective of the heightened vigilance that many ACOAs and spouses of alcoholics display. They become exquisitely attuned to the behavioral and physiological cues that indicate when a parent or spouse has been drinking and trouble may be in store (Gravitz and Bowden, 1985).

- *Thinking/Feeling*:

  This metaprogram reflects whether an individual responds to stress in an unemotional, dissociated manner or an emotional, associated manner. As Gravitz and Bowden (1985) point out, many ACOAs learned as children to avoid feelings—to deny and minimize emotional reactions. Frequently the codependent individual expresses fear of being "out of control"; and the expression of emotions is experienced as being out of control. Nevertheless, when the situation itself becomes out of control, they may react paradoxically with heightened emotional responsiveness.

- *Self/Other Attention*:

  This metaprogram refers to the extent to which an individual attends primarily to his or her own needs or to the needs of the other person, or whether she/he attends to the situation or context and evaluates needs within that context. Again, family system roles are likely to correlate to different patterns. The Caregiver and Placator may sort more by Other, the Scapegoat by Self, the Adjuster by Context.

These descriptions are only suggestive. Each individual has his or her own unique set of metaprograms. It is only by questioning a client that one can determine how she/he operates along each continuum. Determining the operating structure, however, provides valuable insight into how the individual views the world. James and Woodsmall (1988) delineate one other category which indicates a more pervasive pattern of responding to events. This pattern, which they refer to as the Action Level Filter provides additional information regarding the codependent individual. Is the individual primarily Proactive or Reactive? Does she/he view herself or himself as capable of influencing events on a day to day basis? At times the codependent person is likely to act in a very proactive manner, especially when operating in a Caregiver or enabler role within the family system. As the situation becomes more and more out of control, there is apt to be a shift to the reactive mode and a concomitant sense of being the victim, helpless to affect the situation.

ADDRESSING THE ISSUES

The NLP intervention techniques outlined in the other papers in this monograph also can be used quite successfully with codependent individuals. Anchoring, for example, is a valuable tool for helping the codependent client access resources. This section describes ways of addressing the specific issues of control, definition of self, and trust and intimacy, which are so central to codependency. A brief discussion of various techniques is presented in reference to the three clients introduced at the beginning of the chapter. References are included which provide more detailed information about the various techniques.

Control

Client A, B.J., came to therapy to "regain control" over her life, to "control the stress" in her life. She spoke about being "on top of things at work" and with her home and children. Her hands were frequently held in fists, the muscles in her neck and shoulders, tense. When speaking of her alcoholic husband whom she "can't get through to," she bit the corners of her lips. Her body shifted from one side to the other as she said "on the one hand, I feel like I have to take responsibility for managing everything or the girls' life will be chaos, but it's getting harder and harder to keep things going. And I can't get T.J. to get help." As is so often the case with codependent individuals, she believed somehow she "should" be able to control the situation. She was motivated to move away from the stress of the situation. Her words, such as "have to" and "can't" and "should" indicated that she was operating out of obligation or necessity rather than possibility. She remained dissociated from her feelings as she described the situation, and had difficulty remembering pleasant memories from her past or with her children. She expressed two conflicting beliefs, "I have to stay in control" vs. "I am helpless to do anything about the situation."

Dilts (1987) explains that conflicts in belief systems occur when two or more presently existing beliefs lead to behaviors that are contradictory, a situation which often creates a "double bind" for the individual. He points out that the most problematic conflicts occur when the opposing beliefs involve identity issues where there is a negative judgment about oneself.

In order to create an integration of the two beliefs and resolve the inherent conflict, Dilts (1987) developed a six-step process. Briefly the process for Integration of Conflicting Belief Systems involves:

1. Identifying the conflicting beliefs or identity issues;
2. Asking the client to describe to think of himself/herself from each of these perspectives, i.e., in terms of physical representation/characteristics; the image she/he has of each as well as the corresponding voice tone and feelings. Then asking the client to imagine, if possible, that each hand holds one of these representations.
3. Asking the client to imagine that these two representations or parts of himself/herself can communicate with each other, look at each other, and describe what they see;
4. Asking the client to identify the positive intention or purpose of each part or belief and then helping each recognize how the conflict directly interferes with achieving this goal;
5. Having each part identify the resources the other part has that would enable him/her to better attain the goal, and then securing congruent agreement between the parts to combine resources and work together for a common objective; and finally

6. Asking the client to bring his/her hands together while creating a new representation that fully integrates the resources of both parts.

Steps 4 and 5 are the most critical, and this short description can only convey the overall framework for the approach. The impact of the intervention on B.J. was profound. She relaxed the muscles in her face, shoulders, and neck. Her breathing became more regular and deeper. She opened her hands and gestured smoothly with them as she said "I don't have to do everything." a major part of her dilemma had been the desire to maintain the appearance of a normal family with her friends and relatives. After the process she was able to consider ways she could talk to these people and enlist their support. She began attending Al-Anon and participated in a structured intervention with her husband who agreed to enter treatment. Over the course of four additional sessions, B.J. began identifying new choices (Possibilities) and started moving toward her own personal goals.

Another powerful NLP technique was used to facilitate her transition to a life with new flexibility and choices. This technique, the Swish Pattern, developed by Richard Bandler is introduced in his book, *Using Your Brain for A Change* (Bandler, 1985) and delineated in greater detail in *Change Your Mind and Keep the Change* (Andreas and Andreas, 1987). Basically the Swish Pattern involves using an individual's internal representation of a problem situation as a trigger for selecting more resourceful responses or choices in the situation. After identifying the context and the specific characteristics of the problem situation, the client then makes an internal representation of himself/herself having the necessary resources for handling that situation. The client is then directed to replace the first representation with the second one, five times in rapid succession. The technique is an extremely powerful tool for redirecting the way the brain processes information about the previously problematic situation.

By the last session, B.J. was able to identify those things which were actually within her control and said, "You know, it's funny, I really feel more in control now that I'm not trying to run T.J.'s life." By the last session, she could also remember and be associated with feelings from pleasant experiences with her family.

Definition of Self

All three clients described in this chapter had issues around self-worth and self-esteem, but of the three, Client B, K.T. seemed to be at the greatest impasse due to an expressed sense of worthlessness, as Dilts terms the issue (Dilts et al., 1990). K.T. had suffered numerous traumatic incidents, both as a child and in her marriage. She indicated that both her parents and her husband told her repeatedly that she was "stupid" and a "loser." This verbal abuse accentuated the negative imprint effects of the physical abuse. And yet, she also spoke of trying to please everyone in the family. She sorted almost entirely by others and had little awareness of her own needs in a given situation. At the same time she relied on outside approval, which she received primarily in school. She was motivated toward achievement in an academic setting, the one arena in which she had experienced success. She was associated into feelings when she recalled some past experiences, but was dissociated and displayed inappropriate positive affect when describing some of the abusive situations she had experienced (i.e., laughing at herself and the incident). She used words such as "It wasn't such a big thing" to describe what it was like being ridiculed, "I was nothing in our home."

Another of Dilts' belief change interventions helped K.T. regain her sense of self-worth, become more aware of her own needs, and use her own internal reference to assess her own performance. The technique, Reimprinting (Dilts, 1987), is designed to help the individual find the resources necessary to change the beliefs and update the role-models that were formed as a result of the negative imprint experience. In addition, the individual is able to resolve the emotional issues resulting from the incidents and to obtain comfort for the traumatic effects, although these are the secondary by-products of the procedure.

The Reimprinting process which is briefly outlined below, again involves six steps:

1. Asking the client to identify the specific feelings associated with the impasse or limiting belief, and to remember back to the earliest experience with the feeling associated with the impasse; while associated with the early memory, having the client verbalize the generalizations or beliefs that were formed from the experience;
2. Having the client dissociate from the experience as if watching a movie, and asking him/her to verbalize any other generalizations or beliefs that were formed as a result of the imprint experience;
3. Finding the positive intent or secondary gain of the feeling of impasse, as well as the positive intentions associated with the behavior of significant others in the experience;
4. Identifying and anchoring the resources or choices the client and the significant others each individually needed then and did not have but that the client does have now;
5. Having the client replay the "movie" seeing how the experience would have changed if the necessary resources had been available to each individual involved in the event, then verbalizing the new generalizations or beliefs that result from the shift in experience; and
6. Having the client relive the imprint experience with the new resources from the point of view of each of the significant people involved (one at a time) and ending with his/her own perspective and updating or modifying the generalizations that now can be derived from the experience.

After completing the reimprinting process, K.T. expressed a new appreciation for herself, and described an image of herself "singing again," which she had enjoyed before her marriage. The inappropriate affect no longer accompanied her memories of past events. She did, however, express loss and sadness over the childhood she could have had and the marriage she had always dreamed about.

Loss is a common issue among ACOAs in particular. Andreas and Andreas (1988) have developed an effective technique for handling the grief and loss related to the death of a loved one. They also have demonstrated the applications of the technique for handling grief over the loss of a dream or an ideal. K.T. responded very positively to the procedure, and afterwards was able to identify the ways she would be able to incorporate the positive aspect of the "dream" into her future, an extremely powerful aspect of the procedure.

The procedure involves contrasting the representation of the grief object (in K.T.'s case, the lost dream) with the representation of someone (or an ideal) with whom the client maintains a sense of having in the present, whether or not this "presence" exists in reality. The characteristics of the representation of the "maintained presence" are then "mapped across" or transferred to the representation of the lost person or dream. As with all NLP procedures, ecology is a critical part of the technique. The client is asked if she/he has any objections to changing the experience so that it now serves as a present resource. K.T. considered this question very carefully, and then answered, "No, as long as I can remember that I want a different life now. In some ways the sadness was a reminder to me that I don't have to live like I used to." She decided that the new representation still carried that valuable information even though the sadness was no longer there.

In the second part of the procedure, the client is asked to identify the most valuable qualities of the newly transformed relationship. The client is then directed to form a representation of these qualities and to install them into the future. K.T. was able to identify the ways she deserved to be appreciated as a child so that she will better be able to appreciate herself in the future, and the qualities she wants in her future relationships. After a year's follow-up, K.T. has moved to a new town, and is very pleased with a new job in an educational setting.

Trust and Intimacy

Neither B.J. nor K.T. were able to trust others before the belief interventions were performed, yet it was Client C, K.F. who expressed the greatest reluctance to trust others. He also expressed concerns about being able to trust his own judgment about what was best for him. He is married, but had been involved with drugs and alcohol for much of the marriage. During his year of sobriety, he described himself as "unable to connect with anybody, not even M.F. (his wife)." His history of abuse had also left him with unpleasant memories of his childhood, but he reported these primarily in a dissociated manner. He had difficulty associating into any experience fully, whether pleasant or unpleasant. At the same time, he sorted primarily by self, and was usually able to see a situation only from his own point of view. However, he relied on external validation of the quality of his work and on any decisions he made. He said that he had thought his life would be different after a year in Alcoholics Anonymous (AA), but that while he was now sober it seemed "hopeless" that things would ever be better.

The Reimprinting procedure was effective in helping him change beliefs about his self-worth and ability to make a difference in his own life. The resources incorporated into both his younger self and to his parents included "trustworthiness" and he also carried a new belief in his own "trustworthiness" into the future. He also shifted to a greater understanding of others' perspectives, especially his wife's. Nonetheless, he still expressed doubt that he would ever be a success as a graphic artist. Two issues were related to this feeling: (1) his belief that he has the capabilities to be a successful graphic artist and (2) his ability to "trust" his own judgment about whether he is doing a good job. To address the first of these issues it was appropriate to utilize a third belief change procedure, the Submodality Belief Installation Procedure, developed by Bandler (1985) and then modified by Dilts (1987).

The Submodality Belief Installation Procedure is particularly useful in situations in which it is difficult to form new beliefs based on past imprints. Dilts (1987) explains that in order for new beliefs to be accepted by the brain, they must meet certain internal criteria. These criteria often take the form of specific representational qualities such as location, distance and size of an internal image; or pitch, direction, and volume of an internal sound or voice. Both Bandler (1985) and Dilts (1987) term these qualities "submodalities." In the Belief Installation Procedure, these qualities are adjusted so that they correspond to the individual's "submodalities" of a belief. This Dilts procedure again involves six steps:

1. Identifying the new positive belief that the client wants but does not yet have, being sure that the new belief meets the following requirements

    - oriented toward the positive;
    - initiated and maintained through the client's own behavior;
    - testable in sensory experience;
    - preserves the positive by-products and intent of the limiting belief;
    - is appropriately contextualized and will not effect others in the client's life in a negative way.

2. Contrasting the submodalities of the new positive belief with another positive belief the client already has about himself/herself;
3. Adjusting the submodalities of the new belief to match the submodalities of the positive belief she/he already has;
4. If there is interference, identifying the submodalities of a limiting belief the client used to have but no longer believes is true and shifting the submodalities of the interfering belief to those of the former limiting belief;
5. Repeating Step 3 five times, as fast as possible, including Step 4 in the process if necessary; and
6. Asking the client to think about times in the future when this new belief will be in operation.

Another submodalities procedure was used to address the second part of the issue. Andreas and Andreas (1987) outline a procedure for enhancing an individual's reliance on his or her own internal reference experience. After identifying the submodalities of a situation in which K.F. does have an internally referenced set of criteria (personal safety when scuba diving, which also afforded a valuable metaphor for "trusting himself"), these submodalities were transferred or "mapped across" to his judgments about his work. In follow-up conversations K.F. indicated he is working more productively than he has in years, and said, "I am really pleased with my work."

In the area of intimacy, K.F. is still evolving. After completing an Integration of Conflicting Belief Systems, such as the one described with B.J., K.F. resolved the conflict about whether or not he wanted an intimate relationship. He and his wife, M.F. are now engaged in a process of identifying what they want in their marriage, and through NLP, building a compelling future to which they can look forward. K.F.'s motivation is also shifting more and more toward the positive things he wants in all areas of his life.

SUMMARY

NLP concepts provide a valuable framework for understanding the issues of codependency. All too often alcohol treatment focuses primarily on the alcohol-dependent member of the family system. Al-Anon and other self-help groups emphasize the importance of addressing specific codependency issues. Frequently, however, codependent individuals are not even aware that they could benefit from Al-Anon or an ACOA group. Each of the three clients described in this chapter identified reasons other than their relationship to an alcoholic as the impetus for therapy. Therefore, the therapist's awareness of codependency issues and patterns can be crucial. In addition, while self-help groups provide invaluable support, augmenting participation in such a program with specific intervention techniques such as those outlined in this chapter, can greatly speed up the recovery process and enhance the quality of clients' lives. The descriptions of the procedures included in this chapter are only brief outlines. The interested therapist will want to consult the original sources for more detailed information. Hopefully, however, these descriptions are sufficient to convey the impact and power of the techniques.

REFERENCES

Andreas, C. and Andreas, S. (1987). *Change Your Mind and Keep the Change*. Moab, UT: Real People Press.

Andreas, S. and Andreas, C. (1988). Dealing with loss. *The NLP Connection*, *2*, 9-12.

Bailey, R. C. (1986). *The Language and Behavior Profile Manual*. Dallas, TX: BALI Screening Company, Inc.

Bandler, R. (1985). *Using Your Brain for a Change*. Moab, UT: Real People Press.

Beattie, M. (1987). *Codependent No More*. Center City, MN: Hazelton Foundation Press.

Black, C. (1981). Innocent bystanders at risk: The children of alcoholics. *Alcoholism*, *1*, 22-26.

Cameron-Bandler, L. (1985). Unpublished communication.

Dilts, R.B. (1987). Belief systems outline. Santa Cruz, CA: Dynamic Learning Center, Inc.

Dilts, R.B., Hallbon, T. and Smith, S. (in press, 1990). *Beliefs: Pathways to Health and Wellbeing*, Portland, OR: Metamorphous Press.

Gorski, T.T. and Miller, M. (1984). Co-alcoholic relapse: Family factors and warning signs. In *Co-Dependency, An Emerging Issue*. Hollywood, FL: Health Communications, Inc.

Gravitz, H.L. and Bowden, J.D. (1985). *Recovery: A Guide for Adult Children of Alcoholics*. New York, NY: Simon and Schuster, Inc.

James, T. and Woodsmall, W. (1988). *Time Line Therapy and the Basis of Personality*. Cupertino, CA: Meta Publications, Inc.

Subby, R. (1984). Inside the chemically dependent marriage: Denial and manipulation. In *Co-Dependency, An Emerging Issue*. Hollywood, FL: Health Communications, Inc.

Subby, R. and Friel, J. (1984). Co-dependency—a paradoxical dependency. In *Co-Dependency, An Emerging issue*. Hollywood, FL: Health Communications, Inc.

Annotated Bibliography

Chelly M. Sterman, MSW, ABECSW, CAC

Neuro-Linguistic Programming is a young field, barely fourteen-years-old, but its theoretical basis is firmly entrenched in existing systems of human behavior, such as Satir's family therapy, Gestalt Therapy in Fritz Perls' inimitable style, and hypnotherapy with Milton Erickson as its major proponent and the strategic forms of therapy of pioneers such as Erickson, Jay Hayley, and Paul Watzalawick.

This bibliography contains several books which I believe laid some of the groundwork for the existing Neuro-Linguistic Programming (NLP) concepts or which seem to bear a distinguishable resemblance to NLP skills and techniques.

Few of the described works are specifically geared toward alcohol or other addictions. This is the first book dedicated entirely to the topic of alcoholism and other addictions focused on the concepts, skills and strategies NLP has presented in the literature during this last decade. All of the described literature is treatment specific and when these treatment elements are properly extrapolated, they form a firm and logical base for alcoholism counseling in general.

The flow of writing emanating from the NLP community appears boundless and new and updated literature is consistently being published. A significant portion of NLP literature describes business communication applications. These works are not included in this bibliography. What follows is a current sampling of the most interesting treatment oriented literature published in the field of NLP.

Andreas, Steve, and Connirae Andreas, *Change Your Mind–and Keep the Change*, Real People Press, Moab, Utah, 1987.

The two authors have focused their use of NLP skills on advanced submodalities interventions. Strategies for directing clients toward a desired and tenable future are demonstrated with the use of individual timelines, the client's internal representations of his past, present, and future. The discussed submodalities are primarily visual such as size, distance, location, brightness, etc. Old experiences are perceived as a filter for present responses to life events and are used as valuable resources for learning to direct oneself toward the future. The authors contend that NLP involves accessing and resequencing experiences in time and thus making cause-effect connections. Cause-effect beliefs are postulated as vitally important in maintaining a coherent internal world with the individual's perception as self being able to exercise choice in his life. The emphasis of this book is on the client's own experiential base.

The authors define a three-step analysis for successful treatment as containing a future that is appealing to motivate the client, knowledge of cause-effect correlation to determine his action and future pacing with the use of submodalities to actually program these behaviors. Future pacing is a technique used to connect the client's present achievements to future realities.

The authors describe several methods for strategic intervention such as the swish pattern to promote the development of a desired self-image that is attractive and motivating. They elaborate on the criteria that motivates an individual to move towards change. Much emphasis is placed on the ecology of the intervention, the appropriateness of the results in the client's life.

The chapter on compulsions demonstrates several exercises using submodalities which produce a decrease in or a movement toward a more neutral mind state in regard to compulsive behavior. The book furthermore deals with development of improved reality testing using a clear sense of self. Emphasis is placed on successfully accessing internal feeling states with sufficient safety for the client so that these states become a resource in treatment rather than a block for fears preventing the client's movement toward well being. Submodalities remain central to all strategies in this book.

Bandler, R. and J. Grinder, *Frogs Into Princes*, Real People Press, Moab, Utah, 1979.

As the first popular NLP book, *Frogs Into Princes* lays a treatment foundation focusing on the process of therapy rather than the content. The book extensively elaborates on the importance of the use of appropriately matching language in the therapeutic relationship in connection to the client's personal style of accessing information in a visual, auditory, or kinesthetic mode. It demonstrates Satir's, Perls', and M. Erickson's methodic intuitive uses of these processes especially in regard to rapport and modeling skills.

In addition to the use of language, this book details accessing cues in accordance with eye movements, the major categories being V^c—Visual constructed images, V^r—Visual rememberged images, A^c—Auditorily constructed sounds or words, A^r—Auditorily remembered sounds or words, K—Kinesthetic or feeling experiences, and A^d—Digital sounds or "self talk." The authors establish a "most common pattern of eye movements," but acknowledge individual differences in human beings usually based on "other than right-handedness."

The authors describe strategies for installing new behavior patterns by making use of accessing cues, extensively using the anchoring process both of the visual and tonal as well as kinesthetic variety and for future pacing these changes, connecting them to a reality-based immediate future of the client.

A number of specific treatment techniques are described in great detail, such as the visual squash and the reframing technique which consists of pattern identification, several processes allowing for the awareness of internal experiences, creation of a new pattern which adds choices to the individual's internal repertoire, ecology checks, and future pacing.

The authors establish the distinction between reality and the individual's perception of reality, his personal map of the territory. The most significant shift the authors emphasize is the one from content—what is wrong—to a generative or process approach.

Bandler, R. and J. Grinder, *Reframing*, Real People Press, Moab, Utah, 1982.

The foundation for this book is the use of reframing techniques, distinguishing between meaning (content) and context, and providing a step by step theoretical and practical basis for using the context reframe in treatment. Several demonstrations and exercises are presented for negotiating between various internal representations which maintain clients in conflict positions. This is followed by the description of a novel technique for creating an internal integration, sometimes with the use of a newly-established internal part, in the context of a desired outcome. This outcome is presented according to the conditions of well-formedness which consists of (1) Stating the goals of the client in positive, non-comparative terms, (2) Within the client's control to allow for a maximum of personal choice as well as responsibility, (3) In an ecological fashion, which means fitting appropriately within the context of the client's life, and (4) Testable within the client's personal experience, his life in the present and near future.

A foundation is laid for expanding the individual reframing model to a systems basis, demonstrating its use with couples, families, and organizations. Virginia Satir's model is then correlated to the use of reframing in NLP.

A final chapter of this book touches on alcoholism and other addiction treatment. The authors emphasize the sequential nature of internal parts of the addicted individual, noting the fact that the client will generally be either in his addicted part or in the part that wants to be sober/straight and they belabor the significance of negotiating between the internal parts of an individual rather than attempting to eliminate the addicted part in order to achieve an ecological integration aimed at obtaining a lasting positive change.

Bandler, R. and J. Grinder, *The Structure of Magic*, Science and Behavior Books, Inc., Palo Alto, California, 1975.

The *Structure of Magic*, part I was published in 1975 as one of the first NLP publications. The emphasis is still largely on linguistics. The *Structure of Magic*, part II is reviewed later on in this chapter.

In this book, the authors extensively describe the general purpose of therapy within the Neuro-Linguistic Programming model. This purpose consists of four basic elements:

1. Identification of the limits the client has given to his model of the world. This is associated with the client's experience of limited internal choices or and unsatisfactory set of options.
2. Recovery of the missing material by going from surface structure (generalizations) to deep structure (particulars within the client's personal experience and his limits in his map of the world).
3. Reconnecting the client to his personal deep structure experi-

ences by reconnecting the client's linguistic model with the ongoing dynamic processes of life, which allows and motivates the client to take responsibility for this process.
4. Enrichment of the client's model of the world.

This four-part process, according to this book, may successfully be based on what the authors call the meta-model. The meta-model offers explicit direction for the therapeutic encounter, but is not designed to be an exclusive therapeutic technique. Rather, it is generative in conjunction with other forms of therapy, since the meta-model is neutral with respect to the content of the therapeutic relationship.

The processes which specify what happens between the deep structure and the surface structure are the three universal processes of human modeling: Generalization, deletion, and distortion. The clients' maps, their internal representation of reality differ from actual reality by one or more of these universal processes.

The reference structure for the full representation of the deep structure is the full range of human experience. Components of the reference structure for the deep structure are:

- Sensations which originate in the world,
- The personal contribution an individual makes to these sensations as he receives and processes them.
- The way an individual develops a model that differs from the actual world is in the choices he makes while employing the three principles of modeling. This enables each individual to entertain a different model of the world and yet live in the same real world.

The authors postulate that clients live more successfully if they can generate reference structures which contradict choice-limiting forms of the three universal processes of human modeling.

Bandler, R., *Using Your Brain – For a Change*, Real People Press, Moab, Utah, 1985.

This book, consisting mainly of transcripts of Bandler's teaching seminars, sets the stage for movement toward well being versus a focus on the problem state and the ability to create comfort in being responsible for one's own life. The author demonstrates change techniques which are easy to follow and describes the measurable changes that occur in the client as a result of lasting submodalities and sorting mechanisms changes. He further discusses some of the basic human programs such as motivation, learning, and decision making and introduces strategies for changing belief patterns.

The final portion of the book discusses one specific NLP treatment technique, the swish, in detail. The pattern consists of the following components: (1) Identification of the context, (2) Identification of the negative trigger, (3) Creation of an internal representation of the outcome, (4) The swish of content of 2 and 3, and (5) The test for results as well as internal and external congruity (ecology).

Cameron-Bandler, L., D. Gordon, and M. Lebeau, *Know-How: Guided Programs For Inventing Your Own Best Future*, Future Pace, Inc., San Rafael, California, 1985.

The premise of the book is the necessity to create therapeutic conditions that establish a state of mind for the client which allows him to choose to change his experiences and behavior in effective and useful ways. This method is named EMPRINT and is an arrangement of steps or procedures which, if followed, will consistently result in the same outcome. The total of a client's beliefs and internal processes constitutes the client's model of the world which created meaning and subjective experiences. Therefore, this book proposes to deal primarily with changing a client's model of the world.

Cameron describes five fundamental components for successfully changing a less productive model to one that contains the requisite variety for a client's present and future. These components are: (1) Design of a compelling future, (2) flexibility of criteria, (3) relative specificity, (4) choice responses, and (5) correct cause-effect relationships. The therapist then can assist the client in creating a compelling future by designing a motivation strategy which follows these steps: wishing to wanting to planning to doing to having (maintaining).

The remaining chapters define addictions to food, alcohol, and other drugs in the context of these steps an the client's orientation in time, claiming that clients with a dependency or addiction are largely present oriented and that those who manage to shake these problems are able to make transitions to compelling futures. Cameron spends these chapters in a prescription format defining dependencies and addictions in terms of personal restrictions. The five aforementioned components form the designated program for change on a largely cognitive level and this program is postulated as the prerequisite for change. She enlarges this behavior-oriented model of NLP to encompass relationships between adult partners as well as between parents and their children.

Cameron-Bandler, L., *Solutions*, Future Pace, Inc., San Rafael, California, 1985.

This is the only book in the NLP literature to date that focuses exclusively on therapy with couples and families with specific emphasis on sexual dysfunctions. Cameron writes a very readable book using her knowledge of family systems congruently with techniques from Neuro-Linguistic Programming. Relationship disagreements are perceived in the context of inappropriate beliefs about self and partners and the concurrent internal representations of reality coupled with maladaptive behavior.

The book consistently uses the principles of the meta-model to obtain high quality information from the clients. In assessing cognitive behaviors, rapport skills containing elements such as matching, translating, and leading are discussed as well as the function of visual, auditory, and kinesthetic representational systems, which includes the identification of accessing cues and lead systems. Accurate calibration with emphases on client congruity/incongruity elements are discussed before describing the need for and the elements of a well-formed outcome, which consists of five well-formedness conditions in this framework. The process of visual, auditory, and kinesthetic anchoring is described and demonstrated in a variety of specific NLP techniques, both with individuals and with couples. The various change techniques for couples work discussed in the remainder of this book are the "Change History" and an expanded form for working with couples, a set of techniques called V-K Dissociation and V-K Association, the Reframing technique discussed earlier in this bibliography, Overlapping Strategies, the Therapeutic Metaphor, and the consistent use of Future Pacing.

Dilts, R., *Application of Neuro-Linguistic Programming*, Meta Publications, 1983.

In this collection of articles, Dilts describes Neuro-Linguistic Programming as a model of communication having evolved from the works of Perls, Satir, and Erickson and resulting in a behavior model and a set of operational procedures. He describes the basic tenet of NLP as "The map is not the territory" or "People experience the world differently because each person develops his own model of the world through his senses" or "representational systems," primarily the visual, auditory, and kinesthetic modes (VAK). In addition, he emphasizes the skilled use of language and especially predicates as formidable communication tools.

Dilts' ongoing work is in the area of human strategies and belief systems and this book was the first NLP work that attempted to decipher human strategies through analyzing individual representational systems, to describe the utilization of strategies such as decision making and to analyze the modeling and installation process of strategies. In relation to family therapy, the process of getting anchored in calibrated loops is examined and utilized in terms of reintegration. In a positive sense, anchoring connotes the process of associating an internal response with some external trigger so that the response may be reaccessed when appropriate. Techniques Dilts describes in the context of family therapy are future pacing, creating conditions of a well-formed outcome, anchoring in VAK and reframing in addition to developing the Establishment of a Self-Reinforcing Loop with couples. Dilts extensively describes the Meta-Model with special attention to the particular phenomenon of deletion in which important information is eliminated from an individual's experience of reality, leading to a variety of dysfunctional elements in the person's feelings and behavior.

Finally, Dilts postulates the contribution NLP techniques may have on the symptoms of illness and illness itself, quoting several studies on cancer survivors and their general attitudes toward life. Dilts describes NLP's "positive attitude," i.e., the outcome versus problem orientation, the feedback versus failure focus, and motivation strategies using representational systems and accessing cues as helpful in the healing process. He emphasizes personal congruence as the most important aspect of a healthy state and creates a framework for illness as communication. As specific healing strategies he describes multi-level visualization and metaphors in the Ericksonian tradition.

Grinder, J. and R. Bandler, *Trance-Formations*, Real People Press, Moab, Utah, 1981.

This book focuses on Neuro-Linguistic Programming techniques and Erickson's approach to hypnotherapy.

A series of simple inductions combines approaches to skills such as verbal pacing and leading and their non-verbal equivalent, use of overlapping representational systems, and accessing previous trance states with utilizing anchors and anchoring new trance states with the use of analogue marking.

Advanced inductions involve pattern interrupt techniques, overloading and stacking realities. Strategies for dealing with a reaction are described prior to discussing utilization of these methods. Generative change is presented, specifically the six-step reframe technique while in trance. Further utilization techniques involve behavior generators and methods for pain control. Finally, several inductions following NLP principles are presented for use in self-hypnosis.

Grinder, J. and R. Bandler, *The Structure of Magic II*, Science and Behavior Books, Inc., Palo Alto, California, 1976.

The second part of *The Structure of Magic* again emphasizes the use of language as a therapeutic tool.

The authors state that this book is "about communication and change" and extensively discuss human variety in representational systems. They assert that a person's model of the world differs both from the actual world as well as from models created by other people. The authors show how, with the use of predicates, to distinguish and successfully use the client's representational system, which strategy they call "joining the client's model of the world." By identifying the client's representational system(s), the therapist knows which parts of the world are available to the client, i.e., if an individual's model has a visual basis, his inability to respond on the level of feeling is not a form of resistance, but rather an indicator of the limits of his model. Thus, the authors maintain, the initial purpose of the therapist is to assist the client in switching an experience from the representational system which is causing pain and to occur in a form in which the client can better cope. This provides an altered or new set of life choices.

Much emphasis is placed in this book on client incongruity, the different messages the client sends out on a verbal versus a non-verbal level. The authors perceive this as an expression of internal parts embroiled in conflict, with no part managing to be successful and each part sabotaging the other's efforts. Within a client who has conflicting parts there are—at least—two incompatible models or maps of the world. The authors propose a treatment model for dealing with incongruities that consist of the three phases of identification, sorting, and integration.

The second part of the book gives a detailed description of one form of the basic processes of human modeling, the distortion, which consist of three sub-categories:

1. Cause-Effect: the assumption that a specific stimulus causes a specific experience.
2. Mindreading: the belief that you know what someone else thinks.
3. Lost Performative: a value judgment or opinion in which the source of the assertion is missing.

The authors contend that most distortions are rooted in synesthesia or "fuzzy functions," "faulty connections between feel-see, feel-hear, and feel-feel processes." They give pattern-interrupt techniques geared toward reconnecting the client to his actual experience of reality, which is especially useful with distortion resulting from traumatic events. The writers also emphasize the significance of distortions in family therapy.

Gordon, D. and M. Meyers-Anderson, Phoenix, *Therapeutic Patterns of Milton Erickson*, Meta Publications, Cupertino, California, 1981.

Instead of examining Erickson's formal trancework, the authors focus on other significant elements of Erickson's work by using his own verbatim descriptions. Clearly distinguishable patterns following sequences of internal and external behavior appear which become teachable and learnable. The emerging therapeutic skills and strategies make Erickson's legacy comprehensible and manageable within the context of the therapist's own theoretical framework and experiences working with clients. The major components of the sequence used in Erickson's hypnotherapy as described in this book are as follows:

1. the rapport and pacing experience,
2. the sorting skills in the context of the search for appropriate frames for clients' difficulties, a way of making liabilities into assets,
3. specific behavioral interventions based on the concept that the prescription needs to be for naturally occurring behavior and that the smallest intervention you can make generates the most change in the desired direction (less is more).

The authors demonstrate the strategic modes described earlier against specific crises in the family life cycle.

Haley, J. *Uncommon Therapy, the Psychiatric Techniques of Milton Erickson, M.D.*, W.W. Norton and Co., Inc., 1973.

This book describes Haley's experiences with Milton Erickson and his form of working with people in a mode called strategic therapy. Haley describes therapy as strategic if the clinician initiates what happens during therapy and designs a particular approach for each problem. This approach guides the work done during therapy as well as the life of the client once he leaves the therapist's office. Thus, in this form of intervention, the therapist takes responsibility for directly influencing people.

Some key elements of strategic therapy are: (1) encouraging the resistance, (2) providing a worse alternative for the presenting problem, (3) using metaphors, (4) encouraging relapse, (5) encouraging a response by frustrating it, (6) use of space and position, (7) emphasizing the positive, (8) seeding ideas, (9) amplifying a deviation, (10) controlling information, (11) awakening and disengagement, and (12) avoiding self-exploration.

Following families in their journey through life, Haley distinguishes six phases: the courtship period, marriage, childbirth and dealing with the young, middle marriage, weaning parents from children, and retirement and old age.

Henman, J., *Conscious Competence and Other Paradoxes for Adult Children of Alcoholics*, Focus, July/August, 1987.

The author describes his development of an approach geared toward dealing with the paradoxical problem of Adult Children of Alcoholics (ACOAs). The paradox is described as the ACOA having chosen a lifestyle designed for survival at a very young age but continuing this emotionally and otherwise costly lifestyle regardless of new information available in adult life. Henman, using "unconditional respect," challenges, reframes, and alters the "Old Program" and establishes a "New Program" that is more compatible with a present reality. New Program is based on three principles: (1) the intrinsic value of mutual respect for self and others, (2) the belief in a bridge between a conscious mind and the parts of self that have been associated, (3) the belief in the concept of a loving God according to the individual's understanding.

New Program is focused on teaching the client how to be a loving resource for the little child inside and by doing this making it possible for the adult to successfully re-experience the traumas that created the original dissociations, bringing adult resources into play.

Rosen, S., *My Voice Will Go With You*, W.W. Norton and Co., 1982.

This book contains a collection of Milton Erickson's "teaching tales" or metaphors. Erickson, the master of the use of metaphors and language in general intended to influence patients both on conscious and unconscious levels simultaneously. His goal was to positively but indirectly seed suggestions by evoking a variety of emotions. He often relied on playfulness and a sense of humor. The tales frequently follow archetypal patterns, often including the theme of a quest. A number of categories of subjects are described which lend themselves congruently to the use of metaphors. Subjects involve modeling the patient's world and then role modeling the patient's world, indirectly providing the patient with a way out of his dilemma. The metaphors are quite specific in accordance with the client's needs and cover themes such as creating motivation in patients, trust in one's own internal resources, dealing with patient resistance, overcoming habitual limitations, positively shifting the patient's perception of reality (reframing), the value of personal experience, taking responsibility for or charge of one's own life, accurate perception of reality, and being well-informed, and the need for clear personal values and self-discipline.

In the chapter on psychotic patients, the author demonstrates Erickson's principle of creating the most significant change through the smallest intervention.

Erickson is described as a master in setting up situations to achieve a planned purpose and to always create a goal and then work backward toward the problem rather than initially focusing on the problem.

Watzalawick, P., J. Weakland, and R. Fisch, *Change – Principles of Problem Formation and Problem Resolution*, W.W. Norton and Co., 1974.

This book is one of the classics about the use of strategic therapy. It examines how specifically problems arise and are perpetuated in some instances and resolved in others. This form of strategic therapy extensively uses the paradox or double bind to create change in human situations that have reached an impasse and relies heavily on action on the part of the client rather than on insight. The authors emphasize the importance of this action, if the therapy is to be successful, to be applied to the attempted solution – specifically to that which is being done to deal with the difficulty – and not to the difficulty itself. Furthermore, the authors address themselves to second order (or meta-level) rather than first order change. The authors frequently make use of reframing techniques in this context "as a means to change the conceptual and/or emotional setting or viewpoint in relation to which a situation is experienced and to place it in another frame which fits the "facts" of the same concrete situation equally well or even better, and thereby changes its entire meaning."

Yeager, J., *Thinking About Thinking With NLP*, Meta Publications, 1985.

The author lays a framework for the effective use of Neuro-Linguistic Programming (NLP) skills and highlights NLP's far reaching application to human potential. He points out that the need for change indicates the need for a different response from the same stimulus and demonstrates how, with the use of anchoring, a contextual shift can be created to respond to this need. The author establishes that childhood programming teaches an individual how to interpret and give meaning to experiences. He describes how the purpose of the NLP practitioner is to add choice at the point where the person is presented with a stimulus and how a new response potential in the client's repertoire is elicited. The author postulates that as specific change tools, the various forms of reframe are most powerful in their ways of adding meaning to an experience in order to create an expanded behavioral set of responses. Yeager emphasizes that an individual's model determines his flexibility in dealing with life experiences and that NLP's most significant contribution lies in the requisite variety and flexibility it brings to the treatment process.

Index

For Product Safety Concerns and Information please contact our EU representative GPSR@taylorandfrancis.com Taylor & Francis Verlag GmbH, Kaufingerstraße 24, 80331 München, Germany

Batch number: 10725979

Printed by Printforce, the Netherlands